Creation Science:
A Study Guide to Creation!

by
Felice Gerwitz and Jill Whitlock

Media Angels® Inc.
Fort Myers, Florida

Creation Science: A Study Guide to Creation!
Media Angels®, Inc.
Ft. Myers, Florida 33912
www.MediaAngels.com
©1994 by Felice Gerwitz and Jill Whitlock
Revised 1997, 2003.
ISBN # 0-9700385-0-X

Scripture quotations are taken from:
New International Version Bible, Grand Rapids: Zondervan Bible Publishers, 1983.

This book is dedicated to our families, and to our
Heavenly Father whose intervention in our lives has made this book possible.

We would like to thank all the people who prayed and encouraged us during the writing of this book—especially our families. We would especially like to thank Chris Thomas and Paula Holmes, our past editors, and Mary Jo Tate, our current editor, for their time and devotion to making this book a priority. Another special thank-you goes to Frank Sherwin from the Institute of Creation Research for taking the time over the years to read and edit this book. You have truly been a God-send, and we couldn't have done it without you.

Special acknowledgment from Jill: I especially want to thank Dennis Petersen, whose "Unlocking the Mysteries of Creation Seminar" I attended in Coeur d'Alene, Idaho, many years ago when I first became a Christian. He inspired my interest in Creation Science.

Table of Contents

INTRODUCTION

Any comprehensive study of science is going to come up against the "Creation versus evolution" debate. Some maintain that evolution, the idea that life developed randomly from non-living substance, is a purely scientific theory and that Creation is purely a religious viewpoint. The aim of this study guide is to present a scientific approach to Creation as we examine the physical universe and how it came into being.

Throughout the United States and the world, more and more legitimate scientists are considering the possibility that the complexity, organization, and perfection seen in the universe and on the Earth could only have been the result of special Creation by a Divine Designer. This scientist once believed that everything taught in school pertaining to the theory of evolution was pure scientific fact. After careful analytical study of the scientific evidence, I have come to the conclusion that the physical evidence does not support the evolution model, but rather the Creation model.

Scientists will tell you that they are in search of the truth. This is usually the case unless the truth happens to be in opposition to what the scientist holds as firm belief. Belief in the theory of evolution requires as much or more "faith" than does belief or "faith" in Creation. **True science is *observable, testable,* and *repeatable*.** Neither evolution nor Creation can be duplicated in a laboratory, and therefore both are belief systems. I am presenting a scientific argument which demonstrates why the Creation model better fits the observable universe. Christians should never be afraid of science, because science will ultimately prove that the Bible is the true and accurate account of how this incredible world in which we live came into being. I hope your faith in Creation will be strengthened as you pursue the scientific evidence abundantly provided by the Creator of the universe.

Jill Whitlock

Timeline from Creation of Adam to Jacob

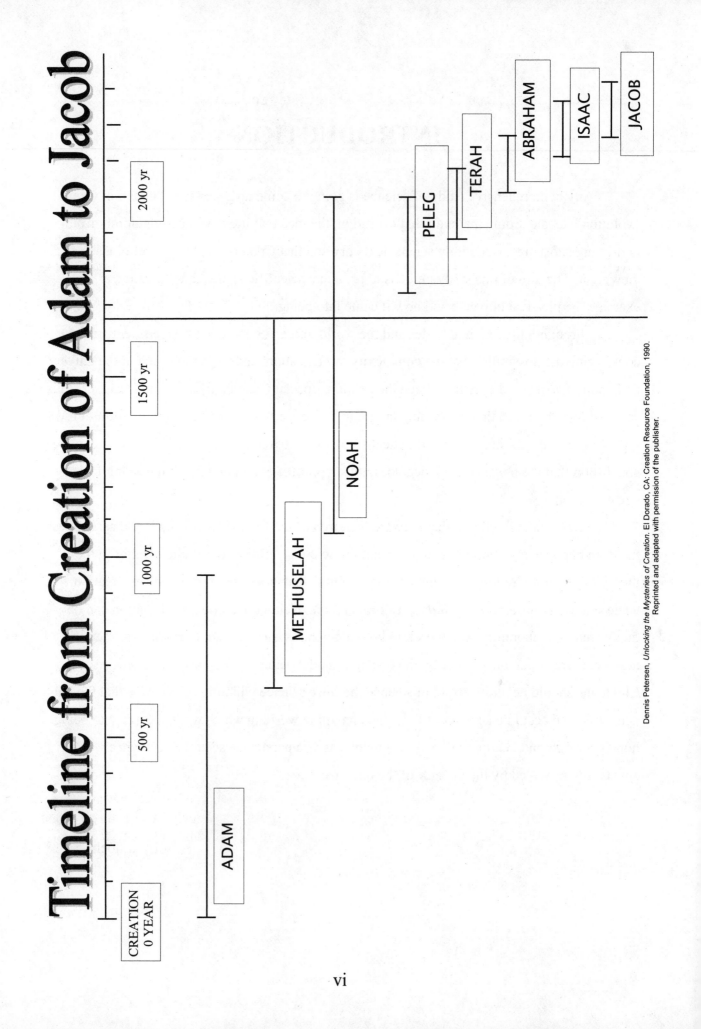

CREATION 0 YEAR

500 yr

1000 yr

1500 yr

2000 yr

ADAM

METHUSELAH

NOAH

PELEG

TERAH

ABRAHAM

ISAAC

JACOB

Dennis Petersen, *Unlocking the Mysteries of Creation.* El Dorado, CA: Creation Resource Foundation, 1990.
Reprinted and adapted with permission of the publisher.

Let's Do a Creation Science Unit!

How much do you know about Creation? Like most of us, you are probably familiar with the Genesis account of the six days of Creation and Noah's Ark. This unit is designed to take you further than you ever thought possible! We have thoroughly researched the topic. (Jill has studied Creation science since 1984!) We have tried to make a technical subject easy to understand and teach.

To make this study useful to teachers of different grades, it has been divided into three levels. The divisions are **kindergarten through grade three,** grades **four through eight**, and grades **nine through twelve**. Another feature is subject divisions, which follow the study outlines to give you some ideas on how to incorporate **reading, vocabulary, spelling, grammar, language arts, math reinforcements, geography, history, science projects, activities, experiments, art,** and **music** into your unit studies. We have included ideas that we believe to be the most helpful. Some of the games and activities are old favorites which have been revised a little to fit the occasion.

A **resource guide** is provided to aid you in obtaining materials; many of the books listed are readily available. Unfortunately most libraries do not carry a wide selection of **Creation science books,** so we list various sources where these materials may be purchased. There is also a guide to Creation science **videos** and **audiotapes.** We have included a **materials list and field trip guide,** as well as pages you may copy: **science experiment sheets** and **materials chart.** We have supplied **Internet** information.

When your child is learning a new scientific concept, make sure you have him re-tell in his own words what he has just learned. For example, if you are teaching about density, you may want to do an experiment which illustrates the concept: float a "toy ark" in water and drop a shell in beside it. Ask, "Which one floats and which one sinks?" A young child may answer, "The boat floats and the shell sinks." An **older child** should be required to explain why: "The shell is denser than the water it displaces, and the ark floats because the weight of the ark is less than the weight of the fluid it displaces." This is a quick way to check to make sure your child is following the concept and not getting sidetracked by the fun!

Creation science is a challenging area to study. Please refer to the detailed **Teaching Outline** in the front of the book, beginning on page 9. This outline corresponds to those in each of the three grade-level divisions, although not precisely. (We have obviously left out some of the complicated points and discussions in the outlines for younger students; therefore, the outlines are numbered differently.) Look for the topic headings when looking for a further explanation in the Teaching Outline. You will easily be able to spot the sections that Felice Gerwitz, educator, and Jill Whitlock, scientist, have written! (*I tried to keep her to the basics, but alas, it was not possible in some areas....*)

With some preparation, your children will soon be sharing with others all that they are learning. They will be able to recognize the difference between beliefs held by evolutionists and those held by Creationists. It is our hope that this unit encourages you and your children to further study the subject and discover the exciting truth of Creation! Are you ready? Let's start our adventure...

Felice Gerwitz

How To Prepare a Unit Study

What is a unit study, and what are the advantages of teaching in such a manner? This is an often-asked question which we will attempt to answer. For additional information, one excellent book that we recommend is Valerie Bendt's *How to Create Your Own Unit Study,* which gives an in-depth explanation of how to plan a unit.

What is a unit study?

A unit study is taking one topic, in this case Creation science, and interrelating all the other subjects into a unified teaching approach. In other words, while studying the topic of Creation science, the children will *read* Creation science books and research materials, *write* assignments relating to what they've read, *spell* words they may have had difficulty reading or writing, *learn* vocabulary words dealing with Creation science, do *math problems* based on scientific principles, read and research *historical periods* relating to Creation and time periods in which noteworthy evolutionists or Creation scientists lived, study *geographical locations* of scientific discoveries and Biblical events (e.g., where Noah's Ark now rests), create *art works* dealing with the flood (such as drawing the animals that went into Noah's Ark), and for *music* play instruments that make sounds similar to those in nature. In other words, all the subjects will relate to the main topic. (The authors suggest that you supplement grammar, phonics, and math with other programs, where age appropriate.)

Why teach a unit study?

The unit study approach emphasizes that reading many books related to a topic, rather than isolated textbooks, encourages discussion and research on the part of the children, therefore making learning more natural and retention of information much more successful. This is ideal for parents with children at different grade levels. It makes teaching much easier. The main area of interest can be taught in a group; then children can work on age-appropriate activities individually. It keeps the family together most of the time, rather than separating children to do their own individual work. It also encourages older siblings to assist younger ones and thereby learn by teaching.

Traditionally, subjects are taught in an isolated manner in textbooks or workbooks with fill-in-the-blank format. Very few, if any, of the subjects are interrelated, and all of the learning is done in an individual manner. Unit studies relate all academic subjects under one main idea and can easily work with one child or a group of children.

Does a unit study cover all of the topics I need to teach in every grade?

Yes and no! It depends on the grade level of your child and what your goals are for your home school. Many children know all they need to know for kindergarten by the time they are preschoolers, leaving the kindergarten year free to implement unit studies on many different topics. Often, as the child progresses, because of all the reading, research, projects, and experimentation that he does, his learning will surpass what is generally considered "normal" for his grade level. Still, if you are concerned about standardized testing, the authors recommend you use these study guides as supplements to your core curriculum. However, in many cases, when homeschool students who have been taught with the unit study approach take a standardized test, they score in the 90+ percentile.

How long does it take to complete a unit study?

Unit studies may be completed in several weeks or studied for an entire year depending on the depth of your coverage of a topic and the varying abilities of your children. For example, we have used our Creation Anatomy study guide in our family as a unit study covering three months. We will use it again as a core subject for high school credit for Anatomy when the time comes. With units you are not bound to a routine of one hour for each subject. The relationships between the topics are natural, and you will often find many subjects are covered without much effort. You will also be free to spend more time on a particularly interesting topic as you see your children's interest level rise in that area. These study guides are meant to be supplemental to your core curriculum, and you can tailor them to meet your family's needs.

How do I get started with planning?

We have done much of the planning for you with our ready-to-go lesson plans (see below). If you are interested in planning your own lessons, the best place to start is with a calendar, paper, pencil, and the **Teaching Outline** in this study guide. Read through the outline and choose the points you wish to cover. You may use the topics provided in each of the three grade levels, or you may utilize them as starters in creating your own outline. The **grade level teaching outlines** are geared for each of three levels: K-3, 4-8, and 9-12. They are not as extensive as the Teaching Outline in the front of the book; therefore, the numerical labels do not correspond exactly. Use the **Teaching Outline** to familiarize yourself with the topic; it is designed specifically to be read by the parent as preparation for teaching the topic. It will give you the necessary information and background to teach the unit. We encourage you to read portions aloud to younger children and have older children read them alone or with you.

As you write your outline or points you want to cover, leave room for additions (you may later run across a book or topic that you want to include). Decide how long you want your unit to take. What months are you considering? Is this time before a major holiday? If so, you may want to do a shorter unit. Is it the beginning of school, summer, or other longer period of time? If so, you may wish to do a more complicated unit or spend more time digging deeper into the topic you choose. Decide what subjects you want to incorporate and what days you will do each. For example you can work on reading, writing, grammar, and math every day, but perhaps science experimentation and history will only be done three out of five days. You may prefer a Mon.-Wed.-Fri./ Tues.-Thurs. type of routine, or if you take Fridays off, your schedule might be Mon.-Wed./Tues.-Thurs. (See sample schedules on page 6.) Remember, it's up to you.

Approximately 6-8 weeks is a good time span for the study of Creation science. We feel this is an excellent preparation to counter secular materials, where it is almost impossible to avoid the evolutionary viewpoint.

How do I use the lesson plans provided?

Included are sample lessons for a six-week study for each grade. You will find these after each outline. Here you will find specific Bible verses to read, as well as science experiments or activities, language arts and spelling, history, music, and art activities mapped out daily for you. You will notice that some areas are left blank for you to include books of your choice. We understand that *not every book* we specify will be available to you. You may not find *any* of the books you are looking for. Do know that the teaching outline gives you the major points you should understand after the end of the lesson. If you do not like the activity we have specified, feel free to omit it and substitute your own! We have supplied a blank lesson plan sheet for you to photocopy.

Go through the age-appropriate outlines and look for the activities and assignments suggested in the lesson plans. If you have a mix of older and younger children, try to find a middle ground as a starting place. Check off the activities that interest you in each subject area. Decide which supplemental books you will need, and plan on obtaining them. Interlibrary loans are able to obtain books from private libraries. Did you know that in most cities you can order library books online and have them ready to be picked up at the checkout desk? What a time saver, especially if you have younger children.

This study contains a list of a greater number of books than necessary so that if you can't obtain one particular book, you may be able to find another. Use the topics as your guide.

This is too overwhelming! Will I be able to implement it all?

Don't become discouraged or feel overwhelmed. It takes one or two unit studies to become comfortable and feel like an "old pro." One way to fit everything in is a day-by-day approach. You may want to do all of the reading and research on day one, geography or history on day two, math and language arts (vocabulary, spelling, and grammar) on day three, science experiments on day four, art and music on day five. Day five can also be used as the catch-up day to finish any work not completed on the previous four days. I highly recommend a "game" day on Friday for grades six and under. This entitles your child to bring out educational games to play on this day.

Decide which books you want your children to read on their own. Many times older siblings can be a great help in teaching the younger ones and will have lots of great ideas for projects. Remember, unit studies have the goal of tying in as many subjects as possible, so you don't need to supplement with a spelling workbook or vocabulary workbook unless your child has a definite need that can't be met any other way. Consider that it might be overloading the kids with seat work and creating frustration when they can't get it all done. (We speak from experience!)

How do I test to find out if my children have learned what I am teaching with the unit approach?

We have found that working closely with our children tells us all we need to know about what they know and don't know. By reading materials orally and then verbally questioning them, we know what needs review and what doesn't. They do many hands-on activities that reinforce previously read materials. For example, in this book there is a discussion of evolutionary principles. One of the points made is how evolution violates the second law of thermodynamics. That in itself sounds very dry and scholarly, yet a follow-up activity, the "Entropy" experiment, presented after the discussion, is a very visual way to reinforce what they have learned. If the children can explain it to you, then you know they understand the concept. After reading all this, if you feel the need to create tests to find out what they know, feel free to do so! You could easily generate oral tests for the little ones, and essay questions for the older ones. One of the great things about homeschooling is the freedom to teach as you wish.

What about co-oping?

Co-oping is teaching a unit study with another family (or several families) and taking time—usually once a week—to work together on projects, experiments, or activities for the entire day. Each family focuses on the unit topic at home during the week by reading books or completing additional projects the co-op will not be covering. The co-op is a way of reinforcing the subjects taught at home with hands-on and group activities. This unit lends itself well to co-ops. There are many experiments that would be fun to do as a group. Still, they can be done just as easily with a single family. A great resource is *Co-Oping for Cowards* by Pat Wesolowski of DP& Kids Productions. Pat's e-mail address is bisb@juno.com, and her website is www.co-oping4cowards.com.

Why teach using a science approach rather than literature or history?

Each of the approaches has its pros and cons. We prefer science because it focuses on experimenting, which encourages creative thinking and exploration on a greater scale than either literature or history. Truly, it is a matter of preference. We have done literature and history as well as science units with our children. Of course we feel that the knowledge of Creation is important to counteract what the secular media is teaching.

We pray that this will help you with unit studies. We believe that learning should be fun for you and your children, while still being educational. When it's fun, hands-on, and messy (especially messy!), the learning experience will stay with them. Try not to get bogged down and become a slave to a schedule (recipe for disaster!). While Jill was living in Washington state, a friend of hers was doing a unit on Washington state history. They traveled all over the state visiting historical sites. After a boat ride to see the orcas migrating, they were so intrigued that they visited the Sea-aquarium and beaches, etc. Soon they realized they were no longer doing a unit on history but one on marine biology. That's the way unit studies should flow!

Suggested Schedule

For those of you who would like help planning a schedule for this study, I have drawn up some thumbnail sketches to use as a basis for planning. Please use these loosely and feel free to add or delete anything you wish. Notice that I have not included times. This is intentional, as there is no way I can know what will work for you and your family. The next page contains a blank weekly lesson plan sheet. Before each grade level you will find weekly lesson plans if you wish for a more detailed chart.

Schedule A

Monday	Tuesday	Wednesday	Thursday	Friday
Bible/Prayer	Bible/Prayer	Bible/Prayer	Bible/Prayer	Bible/Prayer
Suggested reading	Language Arts activities	Suggested reading	Language Arts activities	Suggested reading
Vocabulary, Spelling, and Grammar	Math reinforcements	Vocabulary, Spelling, and Grammar	Math reinforcements	Vocabulary, Spelling, and Grammar
Science activities	Geography/History	Science activities	Geography/History	Science activities
Art	Music	Art	Music	Art

Schedule B

Monday	Tuesday	Wednesday	Thursday	Friday
Bible/Prayer	Bible/Prayer	Bible/Prayer	Bible/Prayer	Bible/Prayer
Suggested reading	Math reinforcements	Suggested reading	Math reinforcements	Suggested reading
Language Arts activities	Vocabulary, Spelling, and Grammar	Language Arts activities	Vocabulary, Spelling, and Grammar	Language Arts activities
Geography/History	Science activities	Geography/History	Science activities	Geography/History
Finish activities	Music	Finish activities	Art	Finish activities

Schedule C

Monday	Tuesday	Wednesday	Thursday	Friday
Bible/Prayer	Bible/Prayer	Bible/Prayer	Bible/Prayer	Bible/Prayer
Math textbook	Math textbook	Math textbook	Math textbook	Math textbook
Reading/Phonics program	Reading/Phonics program	Reading/Phonics program	Reading/Phonics program	Reading/Phonics program
Suggested reading	Math reinforcements	Suggested reading	Math reinforcements	Suggested reading
Language Arts activities	Vocabulary, Spelling, and Grammar	Language Arts activities	Vocabulary, Spelling, and Grammar	Language Arts activities
Science activities	Geography/History	Science activities	Geography/History	Science activities
Music	Art	Music	Art	Music

Lesson Plans

Jacqui

Subject	Monday	Tuesday	Wednesday	Thursday	Friday
Bible/Religion Studies 15-30 min	Bible/Prayer Religion	Prayer Religion		▷	Mass
Creation Teaching Outline 30 min	Day 1 Light & Dark	story 2 Creation	Day 2	Create Lap Book	Finish ▷
Reading Selection 30 min	Phonics	Phonics			▷
Language Arts 10 min	Spelling list of words	Play word game	Spelling list game	incorporate spelling into Lapbook	→
Math Reinforcement 30 min	Math - N-ste singa pou			Add math Page → book	▷
Science Activities and Experiments 1 hr.	Creation	Geo/H+	Creation	Geo/H+ add	Add Sc. Exp + Geo/H+ → Lap Book
Geography/History Ideas 30 min	in history	↓		↓	
Art/Music 15 min	mommy toys & turn on classical music	music	Art	music	Add Art + Mus to Lapbook

CR= Creation Resource   TS= Teacher Selection

Lesson Plans

Subject Date:	Monday	Tuesday	Wednesday	Thursday	Friday

Teaching Outline

Around the world today there are many accounts of how our universe came into being. Here in the United States, two diametrically opposed beliefs are very strongly held and argued by both sides. One is said to be scientific, the other purely religious. Creation scientists look at the universe as having been specially created by God. This view rules out any possibility of evolution occurring. Neo-Darwinian scientists look at the universe as having been formed slowly over millions and billions of years. This view rules out any possibility of Special Creation by an Intelligent Designer.

These two diametrically opposing views cannot be resolved, so the debate continues. However, a belief in evolution actually requires more faith than a belief in specific creation by a divine Creator. Evolution is really more myth and hypothesis. Many points offered in support of evolution have been disproved, as we will show you. More and more scientists are abandoning the theory of evolution for a belief in Intelligent Design and acknowledging that a Creator was necessary. Many of these scientists started out as staunch evolutionists, but with new information and discoveries, they have changed their views. A few of these scientists are: Dr. Paul A. Nelson, a philosopher of Biology; Dr. Dean H. Kenyon, professor of biology at the University of San Francisco; Dr. Michael J. Behe, biochemist at Lehigh University; Dr. Stephen C. Myer, a former evolutionary biochemist at the Discover Institute; Dr. William Dembski, a geneticist from Australia; Ed Macosko, a molecular biologist from the University of California Berkeley; Scott Minnisch, a molecular biologist from the University of Idaho. Geologists, physicists, and scientists already working in the Creation science field include Dr. Henry Morris, Dr. John Morris, Dr. Steve Austin, Dr. Russell Humphreys, Dr. Carl Wieland, Dr. John Baumgardner, Dr. Andrew Snelling, Dr. Larry Vardiman, and many others.

I. Days of Creation

A Day Is a Day — There is much controversy over the meaning of time in the days of the Creation week. Some theologians propose the Day-Age Theory, in which each day represents a thousand years. Others, such as proponents of the Gap Theory, find ways to put long ages into the Genesis account. Most Creation scientists believe the days of Creation were twenty-four-hour time periods. The words used in the text of Genesis clearly indicate that this is so. The definition of the Hebrew word *yom,* which is used in Genesis 1, is "a regular day." The use of the terms "evening and morning" also designates one day. Whenever the word *yom* is used with an ordinal number (1, 2, 3 . . .), it means a twenty-four-hour day. This is a frame of reference that would have been familiar to Moses and his people when he was writing this book for the Hebrews. This same word, *yom,* is used 359 times outside of the book of Genesis to mean a twenty-four-hour day. To the Hebrews, there would have been no doubt as to the meaning of this word: a literal, twenty-four-hour day. God Himself, when writing the Ten Commandments, wrote in stone, "For in six days the Lord made heaven and earth, the sea, and all that is in them, and rested the seventh day" (Ex. 20:11).

The Space-Time-Matter Continuum — "In the beginning God created the heavens and the earth" (Gen 1:1). In this very first verse of the Bible, God establishes the *space-time-matter continuum.* "In the beginning" starts time. God is eternal, but we can only try to understand Him in the limited terms of what we define as time such as minute, day, hour, etc. "The heavens" is the space. That includes our atmosphere, the stars we see in the universe, and the dwelling places of God and the angels. And "the earth" is the matter. Matter and light (energy) are related according to Einstein's theory of relativity where $E=mc^2$ (Energy = mass times the speed of light squared). Here the energy of a substance is related to its mass multiplied by the square of light speed. Nehemiah 9:6 states, "You made the heavens, even the highest heavens, and all their host, the earth and all that is on it, the seas and all that is in them." This leaves nothing out of the days of Creation. God created everything that has ever been. That leaves no room for the Gap theory, the Day-Age theory or any other compromise position that theologians have come up with to try to make the Bible fit into secular science. (See False Concepts page 13.)

Day One: Light and Dark — "God is light" (1 John 1:5). On the first day of Creation, God separated light from dark and day from night. Gen. 1:5 says, "And there was evening and there was morning—the first day." The phrase "there was evening and there was morning" indicates a normal day. Because a day on Earth is measured by one complete rotation, we understand the earth began to rotate. However, there was no sun yet, as it was created on the fourth day. The light came from the presence of God. The Bible repeatedly refers to God and Jesus as light—physical and spiritual light. As Christians we believe Jesus to be totally divine and totally human, one being with two inseparable natures. Science does not have a precise determination of what light is, but it has revealed that light has two natures. Light functions as a wave and as particles. These two functions seem to be contradictory, but both are very real characteristics of light. So too is the character of Jesus, The Light of the World. He was born of a woman and is totally human, and He is the Son of God and is totally divine. (I personally believe that one of the greatest miracles God ever performed was to place His infinite glory in the body of a small baby.)

Day Two: Waters Above and Waters Below — There is currently much controversy over the long-accepted theory of a vapor canopy surrounding the pre-Flood earth protecting it from harmful radiation. A canopy of water vapor at the edge of the stratosphere would also have provided an increase of atmospheric pressure to at least two atmospheres, which would have been beneficial for exceptional growth and rapid healing. A vapor canopy would have caused a greenhouse effect on the planet resulting in a more tropical climate over the entire globe. Some scientists, however, have calculated that such a vapor canopy would have increased the greenhouse effect so much that life would not be possible on earth. Dr. Larry Vardiman, a scientist with the Institute for Creation Research, presented a paper at the International Conference on Creationism in Pittsburgh in August of 2003 entitled, "Temperature Profiles For An Optimized Water Vapor Canopy." In his paper, Dr. Vardiman uses calculations of temperatures beneath a water vapor canopy, varying certain parameters, to show how the greenhouse effect could have been minimized (Vardiman 2003). Also, recent experiments at Texas A & M University have indicated that the long-necked dinosaurs—such as the brachiosaurus, diplodocus, and the apatosaurus—could not have been able to breathe unless there were at least two atmospheres of pressure due to the time it would take for oxygen to flow into their very long necks. Breathing would have required the assistance of double atmospheric pressure.

Waters Above — In the pre-Flood environment, the earth could possibly have been surrounded by a canopy of water vapor. "So God made the expanse and separated the water under the expanse from the water above it" (Gen. 1:7). Picture a bubble of water surrounding the earth causing a greenhouse effect and temperate climate world-wide. (See Section III—Flood Geology and Noah's Ark.) This is not such a strange concept because our neighbor, Venus, is surrounded by a canopy of vapor. Genesis 7:11 states, ". . . on that day all the fountains of the great deep [the waters below] burst forth, and the floodgates of heaven [the waters above] were opened." This was not a local rain shower. The entire heavens were pouring out rain over the entire planet.

Different Pre-Flood Environment — The atmospheric pressure under a vapor canopy would possibly be equivalent to two atmospheres or more. Scientists are aware that increased atmospheric pressure is beneficial to longevity and increases the size of plants and animals. We know from the fossil record that plants and animals grew larger in the past. Mosses that grew two feet to three feet thick in the past grow only a few inches thick today. Fossils of beavers have been found that are over eight feet long, but beavers today average about three feet in length. Fossil dragonflies have been found with wingspans of three feet (imagine one of those hitting your windshield as you drive down the highway!), while today's dragonflies average about five inches.

Advantages of two atmospheres of pressure have been tested with deep-sea divers in hyperbaric chambers. Doubled atmospheric pressure has many benefits: metabolic rates are up, healing is much faster, and resistance to disease increases. Many doctors even prescribe hyperbaric treatments (increased pressure) for some patients during recovery from surgery.

No Storms — Fossils of tropical plants and animals found at both of our polar regions indicate a more temperate environment at one time. The tropical environment worldwide meant that there were no extremes of temperatures—no cold polar regions and no hot equatorial deserts—and thus no rain or storms, which are driven by convection currents caused by temperature differentials (Petersen 2003). Since there were no storms or rain prior to the Flood, God made provision for watering the plants: ". . . but streams came up from the earth and watered the whole surface of the ground" (Gen. 2:6).

The Waters Below — The waters below were the "fountains of the great deep" that God held in reserve for the day of Noah's Flood. The source of the water would have been in reservoirs between the crust and the mantle in an area which geologists now call the Mohorovicic Discontinuity (MOHO for short). This could be what was left when the reservoirs collapsed after the water was released. This water, under the pressure of several miles of rock, could have been at a temperature of 400° F. This super-heated water would not boil because of the pressure and would have shot out at great velocity when released to the surface. It would have had enough velocity to shoot into the outer atmosphere, cool, condense, and begin to rain back down to earth (Creation Science Conference at Clearwater Christian College, 1994).

Day Three: Dry Land and Plants — Genesis 1:2 states that "the earth was formless and void." But it was not meant to stay that way, for God intended to shape it and to fill it. "Formless" means that God had not yet created the landforms, and "void" means that God had not yet filled it with its inhabitants. (See *Unformed and Unfilled* by Weston W. Fields for a word-by-word analysis of Scripture.) In Genesis 1:9 God commanded, "Let the water under the sky be gathered to one place, and let dry ground appear." The waters were in one place, and the land with its plants was, in all probability, all in one place. Even evolutionary geologists theorize that all the continents were once a huge supercontinent which they call Pangea.

Day Four: Sun, Moon & Stars — The lights in the sky were created "as signs and to mark the seasons and days and years, . . . and to give light to the earth" (Gen. 1:14,15). If the sun, moon, planets, and all the stars in the universe were there to give light to the earth and to mark the seasons, then the light from the farthest star had to reach the earth very quickly. Adam and Eve would not have had to wait around for millions of years for light from the stars to reach

11

Earth (Norman & Setterfield 1990; see also *Creation Astronomy: A Study Guide to the Constellations*).

Much of the vast amount of time associated with the age of the universe and evolution comes from the interpretation of modern astronomers. Changes in stars do occur, but they are used as evidence for evolution although it is not certain what is happening. Astronomers have recently reported finding what they call stellar nurseries where they believe stars are being "born." What they see are bright spots that they *assume* are new stars. The problem is that they see only what they are looking for, and they only look for what they already believe in. Evolutionist astronomers have calculated a complex series of theoretical events that they believe occur in the life of a star and that supposedly take millions of years. An article in *Creation ex nihilo* points out that a certain star, FG Sagittae, was observed to change from a blue star at 12,000 degrees Kelvin to a yellow star with 500 degrees Kelvin in only thirty-six years. This observation breaks down the astronomers' stellar series of long ages of time (Wieland 1996).

According to Einstein's general theory of relativity, gravity affects time. This gravitational time dilation, which has been confirmed by observation, shows that clocks located at sea level or low altitudes tick more slowly than clocks at high altitudes. In *Starlight and Time: Solving the Puzzle of Distant Starlight in a Young Universe*, Dr. Russell Humphreys explains that while six regular days were passing here on earth, gravitational time dilation would allow for much longer periods of time to pass at the most distant stars. Dr. Humphreys explains:

> The mathematics of this new theory shows that while God made the universe in six days *in the earth's reference frame* (Earth Standard Time, if you like), the light had ample time *in the extra-terrestrial reference frame* to travel the required distances. None of these time frames can be said to be "God's time," since the Creator, who sees the end from the beginning (Isaiah 46:10, Rev. 22:13, John 8:58, and more) is outside of time. Time is a created feature of His universe, like matter and space. It is interesting that the equations of GR (general relativity) have long indicated that time itself had a beginning (Humphreys 1994).

An analogy for this theory of light from distant stars is that they move much like a line of marchers in a band as they turn a corner. The person on the inside of the corner (Earth) takes tiny steps and covers a very short distance. In the same amount of time, the marcher on the farthest end of the line (distant stars) must take very large steps and cover a much greater distance in the same amount of time. If you used the same increments to measure the time and distance traveled by the marcher on the inside of the corner, then the marcher farthest away would look as if he had been traveling a long time. Another explanation suggests that when God said "Let there be light," the speed of light was infinitely fast, but it has slowed down over time following the graph of a parabolic curve. We don't have all the answers; that is why faith in God's Word is required.

Day Five: All Fish and Birds — "So God created the great creatures of the sea and every living and moving thing with which the water teems, according to their kinds, and every winged bird according to its kind" (Gen. 1:21). This means that God has created everything complete and whole. No further "evolutionary improvements" were needed. All living things were genetically perfect at Creation. In fact, all living creatures reproduce after their own kinds so precisely that a Swedish botanist, Carl Von Linne, better known as Carolus Linnaeus, devised a classification system for plants and animals. In 1735 he published a book called *Systema Naturae* (The System of Nature) in which he explained this identification system of two Latin names, one for genus and one for species. Because this system simplified scientific classification, it was quickly accepted and is still in use today. The reason Linnaeus was able to classify living things was because they reproduce very precisely. If plants and animals were constantly changing into something else, a classification system would be meaningless. Plants and animals maintain their kinds because they were complete and fully functional at Creation according to Gen. 2:1, "Thus the heavens and the earth were *completed* in all their vast array" (emphasis added).

Day Six: All Other Animals . . . — "Let the land produce living creatures according to their kinds" (Gen. 1:24). On Day Six, God made all the land-dwelling animals and man. God created all the kinds of animals and gave Adam the task of naming them. God made everything from insects to elephants and made each to reproduce after its own kind. God even made the dinosaurs. I believe that Adam could have named them dragons and that they were called dragons throughout history until the mid-1800s, when scientists began giving them fancy scientific names. It was a Christian anatomist who was also a Creationist, Sir Richard Owen, who gave these creatures the name "dinosaur," which means "fearfully great lizards." Dragon legends are found in nearly every civilization. Ancient books tell of using dragon parts for medicinal purposes. Oriental civilizations have long used dragons in their art and books. Ancient Chinese stories tell of dragons being bred to pull the Emperor's chariot. England has the legend of St. George slaying a dragon. Stories of Gilgamesh and Beowulf slaying dragons have come down through history. These are just a few examples of eyewitness encounters with dragons or dinosaurs. Dragons are mentioned in the Bible under the names "behemoth" and "leviathan." Fascinating descriptions of these animals are found in Job 40:15-41:34. These verses sound like a reasonable description of dinosaurs. In Job 40:15-24, God speaks about the behemoth, calling him "chief in the ways of God." Job 40:17 says the movement of the tail was compared to a cedar tree; therefore, this cannot be a description of a hippo or an elephant, as sometimes suggested. In Psalm 104:26, David writes about leviathan. (Read all of Psalm 104.) He knew that men were sailing in ships at the same time as leviathan was frolicking in the sea. This is another eyewitness encounter. Isaiah speaks of leviathan as the dragon of the sea (Is. 27:1). Job 41:18-21 describes leviathan as a fire-breathing creature with terrifying teeth and scales like armor. This cannot be a whale, as is commonly thought.

And Then Man — "Then God said, 'Let us make man in our image'" (Gen 1:26). Being made in the image of God means that man was given a spirit. God is a Spirit Being, and to commune with Him, man was made a spirit being. The plants have life but no soul (mind, will, emotions). Animals have life and soul, but no spirit. Only man has been given a spirit in the image of God (Morris 1991).

I have read Genesis many times, but it wasn't until recently that I noticed something that I thought was very interesting about God's Creation. God "spoke" and there was light. He "spoke" and divided the waters. He commanded the water to be in one place and the land to be in another place. God "spoke" and commanded the land to produce plants and the water to bring forth life abundantly. Then He "spoke" and commanded the earth to bring forth all living creatures and all things that creep on the ground. But when God created man, He got very personally involved. He got down in the dirt and formed man from the dust of the ground and breathed His own breath into his nostrils. God did not get that personally involved with anything else in all of Creation.

II. False Concepts

Evolution — Evolution is not a proven fact (as the late evolutionist Stephen J. Gould claimed it is) and therefore it should not be promoted dogmatically as fact. This

unsubstantiated hypothesis of evolution is based on a view that man came from lower life forms that in turn came from non-living substances. Evolutionist Julian Huxley gives the following definition:

> Evolution is a directional and essentially irreversible process occurring in time, which in its course gives rise to an increase of variety and an increasingly high level of organization in its products. Our present knowledge indeed forces us to the view that the whole of reality is evolution, a single process of self-transformation (Creation, 1995).

However, the theory of evolution has been used as more than just a mechanism for change. It is an idea whereby man can decide what is *truth*. This idea which rejects Creation and God as the Creator also allows men to reject God's Word as truth.

Evolutionary geologists encounter an enigma in the very first layers of sedimentary rocks found on the earth, the Cambrian strata. They are at a loss to explain the sudden appearance of creatures from all phyla appearing fully formed and fully functional with no prior transitional forms ever found. They even call this sudden appearance of life "The Cambrian Explosion." There is essentially an explosion of all types of life forms in the lowest stratigraphic layer, the Cambrian Formation. Everything from protozoans, worms, sponges, gastropods, and echinoderms to the extremely complex creature called the trilobite are found suddenly in the Cambrian strata with no transitional forms below there. The trilobites had incredibly complex eye structure that would have given them vision superior to what many animals have today. The most shocking thing for evolution is that bone-bearing animals, the vertebrates, are also present in the Cambrian strata, with no transitional forms below. Here we see pelecypods, bryozoans, corals, starfish, sea urchins, and completely formed vertebrate fish. This does not fit the evolution story.

The physical evidence in the geological record does not support the hypothesis of evolution. No geologist can put his hands on even one transitional fossil. Neither evolution nor Creation can be proven by observation or by experimentation. If evolution were real and had actually occurred, then we should <u>not</u> be able to recognize any organisms in the fossil record. Darwin himself said that the fossil record was his greatest problem. Read the sixth chapter of *The Origin of Species* where Darwin discusses the problem of the fossils. All types of organisms, including vertebrate fish, have now been found in Cambrian rocks, which are the oldest sedimentary rocks. The geologic column was invented by evolutionary geologists to show the presumed evolutionary relationships of animals and plants. The ages assigned to the geologic column were for the purpose of supporting evolutionary claims. The present-day geologic column with its "evolutionary progression" of life was established 100 years before radiometric dating was invented. (See section IV.) The total geologic column may only exist in a very few places on earth (Woodmorappe 1993).

The geologic column was deliberately constructed by evolutionists from various unconnected sections of stratigraphic layers to show an alleged progression of life. An *Answers in Genesis* article reveals:

> The notion that the earth's crust has an "onion skin" structure with successive layers containing all strata systems distributed on a global scale is not according to the facts. Data from continents and ocean basins show that the ten systems (the standard Geologic Column) are poorly represented on a global scale: approximately 77% of the earth's surface on land and under the sea has seven or more (70%) of the strata systems missing beneath; 94% of the earth's surface has three or more systems missing beneath; and an estimated 99.6% has at least one missing system. Only a few locations on earth (about 0.4% of its area) have

been described with the succession of the ten systems beneath (west Nepal, west Bolivia, and central Poland). Even where the ten systems may be present, geologists recognize the individual systems to be incomplete. The entire geologic column, composed of complete strata systems, exists only in the diagrams drawn by geologists! (AiG website)

Theistic Evolution — This theory proposes that God started the evolutionary process and that when primates evolved into man, God placed His Spirit in the first man, Adam. However, this theory has difficulty trying to explain how Eve came from Adam's side. Did some female ape evolve coincidentally at the same time? Furthermore, since Romans 5:12 states that death entered in because of one man's sin, there could be no death until Adam sinned. Therefore there could not have been millions of years of animals that were born and died prior to Original Sin. In fact the original Gospel message is found in Genesis 3. Adam and Eve had covered themselves with leaves, but God made garments for them with some animal skins. This was the first blood sacrifice to cover sin. The Bible is not specific about what animal was slain for its skin, but it could have been a lamb. Perhaps it was a spotless little lamb that Adam and Eve had played with and loved. This would have been a startling picture to Adam of the horrors of sin, and a type of Jesus, the Lamb of God, yet to come..

Day-Age Theory — This theory attributes long periods of time to each day in the Creation week, but does not explain many of the things that are seen in the geological column or the order of their appearances. For instance, the plants appeared on Day Three but the sun did not appear until Day Four, allegedly millions of years later. Careful examination of the Day-Age theory exposes it as a feeble attempt to make the Bible fit into science. The reason many of these theories develop is because many theologians fear science. They take science (man's knowledge) and try to make the Bible fit into it, rather than take the Bible (God's Word) and demonstrate how true science continues to concur with the Scriptures.

The Gap Theory — This concept hypothesizes millions of years between Genesis 1:1 and Genesis 1:2. It attributes the formation of the geological features and the fossil record to this inferred time period. Gap theorists believe there were animals and a whole race of people (which they call the Pre-Adamic race) who lived long before Adam. God then judged these people and sent a flood to destroy the earth, after which He started over again. This is in direct contradiction to the literal words of Scripture. God very clearly states in His Ten Commandments that He created everything in six regular days: "For in six days the Lord made the heavens and the earth, the sea, and **all** that is in them, but he rested on the seventh day" (Ex. 20:11). The Psalmist states in Psalm 119:160, "From the beginning, **all** your words are true." That includes Genesis 1:1, "In the beginning. . . ." As God worked through the Creation week, He would look around and see that it was good. In Genesis 1:31, He sees all that He has made and calls it *very good*. How could God, "who is not a man that He should lie," call His Creation *very good* if Adam and Eve were walking around on billions of dead animals and people who had lived before? This theory is also contrary to Romans 5:12, which states that death entered because of one man's sin. There cannot be death before there is sin.

Compromise: All of these self-described "Christian" positions compromise the Word of God to accommodate a geological timetable that has been shown to be less than accurate. In fact, if there was death before there was sin, then the message of the Cross is foolishness. The just judgment of God requires death as the punishment for sin. Why was it necessary for Jesus to die, unless it was because of Original Sin (rebellion) in Genesis? Jesus recited His heritage all the way back to Adam; so to Him, Adam was a very **real** person, not a myth.

Jesus stressed the importance of believing what was written by Moses in Genesis and elsewhere in the Old Testament many times. In John 5:45-47, Jesus says, "But do not think I will accuse you before the Father. Your accuser is Moses, on whom your hopes are set. If you believed Moses, you would believe me, for he wrote about me. But, since you do not believe what he wrote [the first five books of the Bible], how are you going to believe what I say?" These words spoken by Jesus reinforce the importance of believing all of God's Word. Jesus stressed that an understanding of Genesis and the rest of the Old Testament was necessary to understand Him in Luke 24: 25-27,44: "He said to them, 'How foolish you are, and how slow of heart to believe all that the prophets have spoken! Did not the Christ have to suffer these things and then enter His glory?' And beginning with Moses [author of Genesis] and all the Prophets, He explained to them what was said in all the Scriptures concerning himself."

The following list is a sample of some of the 100+ times that Jesus referred to Genesis:

Matthew 19:4	Genesis 1:27
Matthew 19:5	Genesis 2:24
Matthew 19:26	Genesis 18:14
Matthew 23:32	Genesis 15:16
Matthew 23:35	Genesis 4:8
Matthew 24:37	Genesis 6:3 & 7:1
Matthew 26:24	Genesis 3:16
Matthew 26:52	Genesis 9:6
Matthew 13:23	Genesis 26:12
Matthew 13:31	Genesis 1:11-12
Mark 4:31-32	Genesis 1:11-12
Mark 9:12-13	Genesis 3:15
Mark 10:6	Genesis 1:27- 2:24
Luke 7:44	Genesis 18:4
Luke 10:15	Genesis 11:4:4
Luke 11:51	Genesis 4:8
Luke 13:18	Genesis 1:11-12
Luke 13:29	Genesis 28:14
Luke 15:20	Genesis 45:14 & 46:29
Luke 17:26-27	Genesis 6:12-13
Luke 17:29	Genesis 19:24-26
Luke 22:53	Genesis 3:15
Luke 16:29-31	Refers to Moses and the Prophets
Luke 24:25-27, 44	Refers to Moses and the Prophets
John 1:51	Genesis 28:12
John 5:45-47	Genesis 3:15,12:3, 18:18, 22:18
John 7:21	Genesis 17:9-10
John 8:35	Genesis 21:10
John 8:44	Genesis 3:1
John 8:56	Genesis 22:17-18

III. Flood Geology and Noah's Ark (For a more detailed study, see *Creation Geology: A Study Guide to Fossils, Formations, and the Flood.*)

Ark Design — The Ark was designed by God (Gen. 6:14-16). The dimensions of this remarkable boat have recently been shown to be the most stable configuration for any floating structure. A program on PBS (May 18, 1994) showed scientists testing scale models of various types of ocean-going vessels. Of all the models tested, the one with the same ratio of dimensions as the ark proved to have the most stable configuration. Once again, God knew what He was doing. The ark was the first of its kind. With dimensions of 450 feet long, 75 feet wide, and 45 feet high, the capacity of this boat would have been adequate to care for the animals, Noah and his family, and all the food storage. The same ratio of dimensions has been used for a hundred years on ships like the *Great Britain* and the *Great Eastern,* which were built for stability. Ships like the *Queen Elizabeth II* have a different ratio of dimensions because they are built for speed.

John Woodmorappe has written an excellent book that logically and scientifically addresses many questions associated with the ark, such as available space, waste management, food supply, living conditions and much more. His calculations allow for the animals to fit in one-third of the ark, allowing two-thirds for food storage and Noah's family. He shows that the median-sized animal would be about 200 grams, about the size of a large rat (Woodmorappe 1996).

Stories of a man and his family surviving a great deluge with a large number of animal aboard a very large boat persist throughout many cultures. The Mayans, the Incas, the Aztecs, and the Chinese all have flood stories. Ancient Sumerian writings go into great detail about Noah's family and the Flood. The Greeks remembered Noah as Nereus, the "Wet One." Nereus (Noah) is also referred to as the "Sea Salt Old Man" or "The Old Man of the Sea" and is pictured on a large number of vases. Robert Bowie Johnson, Jr. explains in *Athena and Kain*:

> Hesiod wrote in the *Theogony*, "And Sea begat Nereus, the eldest of his children, who is true and lies not: and men call him the Old Man because he is trusty and gentle and does not forget the laws of righteousness, but thinks just and kindly thoughts." In Genesis 6:9 we read: "Noah is a just man." The memory of Noah's Flood, deeply rooted in the minds of the ancient Greek artists, inspired thousands of vase paintings related to it. . . . The sculptors in Athens even went so far as to depict the Flood and its aftermath on the west pediment of their most treasured temple, the Parthenon (Johnson 2003).

Ancient Sanskrit uses the term *Manu* frequently. In ancient Indian traditions Manu was also the name of a flood patriarch who built an ark and saved eight people. It is very likely that Noah and Manu were the same person. *Ma* is the ancient word for water. The Spanish *mar*, the French *mer*, and the Latin *mare* all mean sea. The name of most Japanese ships ends in the word *maru*. The following quote shows how the Sumerians seem to refer to Noah:

> The name *Anu* appears in Sumerian as the god of the firmament, and the rainbow was called "the great bow of Anu," which seems a clear reference to Noah (note Genesis 9:13). In Egyptian mythology *Nu* was the god of waters who sent an inundation to destroy man kind (Sage 1980).

Fountains of the Great Deep — ". . . On that day all the fountains of the great deep burst forth [these were the 'waters below' that God held in reserve for this day] and the floodgates of the heavens were opened" (Gen. 7:11). The waters below would have been under tremendous pressure and shot up into the air with great velocity. The reservoirs for the fountains of the great deep would have then collapsed when the hydrostatic pressure was removed. There is a zone called the Mohorovicíc Discontinuity, or the MOHO, that marks the separation of the crust and the mantle within the earth. This could be what was left from the fountains of the deep after the reservoirs collapsed.

Geologic Formations — Most geological formations we see, such as the Grand Canyon, were formed during the Flood or shortly after. (See *Creation Geology: A Study Guide To Fossils, Formations, and the Flood*). The "geologic column" actually shows environmental zones at the time of burial, not ages of evolution. In many locations around the world, the supposed geologic column is out of order. From his work in the Grand Canyon, Steve Austin of The Institute for Creation Research has data showing how radiometric dating results in an "assumed" age of 1.07 billion years for the Cardenas Basalt at the bottom of the canyon and 1.34 billion years for the Quaternary basaltic lava flow on the Uinkaret Plateau at the top of the canyon (Austin 1994). How could the layer on top, which was laid down last, be older than rocks at the bottom that were laid down first? Dr. Austin's challenges to radiometric dating and to an old age for the canyon are well supported in his book, *Grand Canyon—Monument to the Flood*.

The fossils found in strata in the geologic column support the Flood concept. Most geological sedimentary structures would have been formed while they were still very wet underneath the water. There would have been a tremendous hydrostatic head (pressure generated by the weight of the water) under the Flood waters. One cubic foot of water weighs about sixty pounds. The sediments would have been unconsolidated, or in the plastic phase, not brittle, and would have folded and shaped easily. Just outside of Denver, Colorado, is Red Rocks Amphitheater, which is made out of a natural formation of vertically tilted red sandstone. I remember that the first time I went there to see a concert, all I wanted to do was study the beautiful example of cross-bedded sandstone in the rocks. It was very obvious that all that massive amount of rock was actually wet sand that had been laid down under water. About sixty miles to the east, these highly tilted rocks, called the Lions Formation, flatten out and are 5000-6000 feet underground and are oil-bearing.

Aquatic Sediments — Water-lain sediments and aquatic fossils on every mountain top indicate that the entire Earth was under water. Even the highest mountain ranges in the world show evidence of materials laid down under water. The Tibetan Plateau, which is three miles high, is covered with 750,000 square miles of sediment, thousands of feet thick. ("The waters rose greatly on the earth, and all the high mountains under the entire heavens were covered" [Gen. 7:19].) The pre-Flood mountains were probably not as high as the present ones. I remember that on every field trip we ever took in college, the professor would tell us that we could find aquatic fossils on the mountain because it was once a lake bed. It wasn't until I was lecturing several years ago that I realized that the *whole earth* was a lake bed during the Flood! And relative to the mountains, the ocean basins have deepened, perhaps due to the collapse of the reservoirs of the fountains of the deep. As the ocean basins deepened, the receding waters filled them as they carved the land, forming the dendritic patterns and sediment gravity flows, and burying massive amounts of animals in the process. (See Section III—Submarine Canyons for evidence for the deepening of the ocean floor.)

Earth's Axis Tilts — It has been postulated that the earth's axis may have been perpendicular or at least closer to perpendicular than today. Chapter Ten of *It's A Young World After All* provides some very intriguing observations about the evidence for the occurrence of axial tilting (Ackerman 1993). If a vapor canopy surrounded the earth, it would have produced a greenhouse effect globally, with or without axial tilt. The climatic conditions would have been much more temperate worldwide. Alligators, palm trees, and other tropical plants have been found frozen in the tundra at the North Pole. Thick coal beds are found in Antarctica, which means lush plant life once lived there. An entire redwood forest was discovered under the ice in Antarctica (Peterson 2003). Once the earth's axis tilted into its present angle of 23.5 degrees, seasons occurred for the first time. The equatorial regions became hotter, and the polar ice caps formed.

Seasons — We experience seasonal changes because of the tilt in the earth's axis. The earth also wobbles on its axis. When the earth is tilted toward the sun we have summer, and when it is tilted away from the sun we have winter. Our earth is actually closer to the sun in the transitional seasons of spring and fall. The Southern Hemisphere experiences the opposite seasons to the Northern Hemisphere. Evolutionists have a difficult time explaining the perfect tilt of our axis. The earth's average tilt is twenty-three and one-half degrees. If the tilt were twenty-six degrees, the poles would melt and flood much of the land. If the tilt were twenty-two degrees, the equatorial deserts would expand and the polar ice caps would enlarge. Also, the planet is at the perfect distance from the sun for life to exist. This is clearly by design, not by chance!

The Ice Age and Polar Ice Caps — The polar ice caps and the solitary Ice Age were caused as a result of the Flood of Noah. When the waters in the fountains of the great deep shot into the stratosphere, it would have added a great deal of heat to the already warmer oceans. All the volcanic activity and the movement of the crustal plates would also help to feed in more warm moisture and, as a result, produce warmer, wetter winters with the heavy snowfall needed (Morris 1993). This would have allowed the ice caps to form. The Poles did not form over millions of years of precipitation. Dr. John Morris, president of the Institute for Creation Research, writes:

> Furthermore, the land surface at the end of the Flood was little more than a mud slick, and would have reflected solar radiation without absorbing much heat. The large temperature difference between ocean and land, and coupled with strong polar cooling, would cause intense and prolonged storms.

> Finally, the late and early post-Flood times witnessed extensive volcanism, as the earth struggled to regain crustal equilibrium. This would cloud the atmosphere, bouncing incoming solar radiation back into space—thus, colder summers.

> More evaporation, warmer winters, more intense storms, and colder summers: The result? An "ice age" which would last until the oceans gave up their excess heat, the volcanism lessened, and vegetation was re-established. This likely would take less than one thousand years following the Biblical Flood (Morris 1993).

Evidence for Worldwide Flood — The physical evidence seen all over the world fits the Flood interpretation. Neither Creation nor evolution can be proven; therefore, both are belief systems. A good scientist will examine the data and then draw a conclusion (the good ol' scientific method). Evolutionists have their own pre-conceived idea of physical processes and try to make their observations fit their conclusion, rather than drawing a conclusion from what is observed. I was an evolutionary geologist for ten years, always believing what I had been taught. After carefully studying the evidence from secular and Christian sources, I am now a Flood geologist and a Young Earth Creationist, and I am fully persuaded that the earth is young and the geological formations fit into the Flood model.

Gills of Fish Preserved — There are numerous fossils of fish in the swimming position with fins extended and gills exposed. Gills degenerate within a few hours after death of the fish, so preservation of gills in a fossil is very significant. Their preservation indicates *very rapid* fossilization. There are many specimens of fossilized fish with smaller, undigested fish in their stomachs. There is even a fossil of a fish with another fish in its mouth. That fish didn't even have enough time to swallow its dinner before it was very rapidly buried. It simply did not take long periods of time for fossils to form. Fossils of bugs with their wings spread as in flight are also found, which indicates the bugs were very rapidly buried. This is an enigma to evolutionists.

Rapid Burial — Preservation of fossils occurs only when their burial is very rapid and exposure to oxygen is stopped (anaerobic conditions). A dead animal left out in the open will decay and leave no fossil or print. Vast fossil graveyards are found in many locations. It has been estimated that the Karoo Formation in South Africa contains the fossils of 800 billion vertebrates, including reptiles and mammals. Many of the animals buried here represent groups that are not normally found together in nature. How could all these billions of animals become buried together at one location? Did they all get up and decide to walk over there and die at the same time? Of course not. There was probably a large depression there into which these animals were washed as the water receded after the Flood. This preservation indicates rapid burial. In contrast, of the millions of bison that were slaughtered in North America, none are preserved because they were left exposed on the surface to the elements, scavengers, and oxygen, and they decayed.

Submarine Canyons — Submarine canyons are another evidence of rapidly receding waters. Great underwater canyons found around every continent in the world indicate a rushing and gouging of water and strong sediment gravity flows. (When I was studying this in college sediment gravity flows were called turbidity currents.) As the oceans' basins subsided, the waters ran off into the deeper basins, scouring out these submarine canyons. The ocean basins collapsed after the fountains of the deep burst forth. The hydrostatic pressure was no longer there to hold them up, so the sea floors collapsed. Sea level is now lower, and relatively, the land masses appear to be higher than prior to the Flood. Guyots are table mountains 5,000 feet under the sea with sandy beaches and coral reefs on them. Sandy beaches are formed at sea level, and corals have a limited range of depth at which they can grow. These are the evidence that the guyots, which are now 5,000 feet below sea level, were once at sea level; therefore, the ocean basins have deepened.

Plate Tectonics and Continental Sprint — Shortly after the Flood, the land mass began to divide, probably due to the tremendous stresses placed on the supercontinent during the Flood. Because the land masses were now separating, some animal and plant variations became isolated on certain continents. (It is entirely feasible to say that kangaroos and polar bears once lived in Turkey, because all animals that survived came off the Ark on Mount Ararat in present-day Turkey.) Then about one hundred years later, according to Biblical chronology, during the time Nimrod was building the Tower of Babel, "One was named Peleg, because in his time the earth was divided" (Gen. 10:25). God not only divided the land physically, but also by confounding the languages at the Tower of Babel (Gen. 11:1-9).

Some have argued that there would not be enough energy 100 years after the Flood to have caused crustal plate movement. However, modern-day earthquakes release their energy, and their subsequent aftershocks can occur years later, and scientists still call them aftershocks of that particular earthquake. Yes, considerable energy would have been released when "the fountains of the great deep burst forth," but it is conceivable that not all the energy was released at that time. Perhaps the movement of the crustal plates that began with the Flood were much more evident to the new inhabitants of the earth during the time Peleg was born.

Magnetic Reversals — On a related topic of magnetic reversals recorded in the rocks extending out from the Mid-Atlantic Ridge as the continents moved apart, I want to clarify something. When I wrote my thesis on this topic in 1975, all the research indicated that the rocks of the Mid-Atlantic Ridge showed that the poles of the earth's magnetic field had repeatedly

20

switched polarities. This means that the North Pole and the South Pole would have reversed their polarities many times over. This would have created total havoc for any life forms in the planet. Recent investigations into these so-called magnetic reversals show that actual reversals do not exist. When the scientists who originally recorded their findings about these magnetic fluctuations plotted their results, they noticed the magnetic field strength would be at a higher level and then at a lower level, higher, lower, and so on. For some reason, someone decided that they would draw a line through the approximate middle of this data and declare that any reading above this line would be a normal polarity and any reading below this line would be a reversed polarity. In actuality there is no reading of the magnetic field in the rocks that indicate the poles were ever reversed. There are fluctuations in the strength of the magnetic fields, but no reversals.

IV. Evidence for a Young Earth

There are numerous indicators of the age of the earth. The majority of them, about 95%, indicate a much younger age for the earth than is suggested by the theory of evolution. The major indicator of an old age for the earth used by evolutionary scientists is radiometric dating, which has many problems associated with it.

Problems with Radiometric Age Dating — Within the last several years, radiometric age dating has proven to be extremely inaccurate. The theory is based on three false assumptions: (1) There is only 100% parent element in the beginning and no daughter product. This assumes that, for instance, in the ^{14}C-^{12}C series the unstable ^{14}C, which is the parent element, exists and none of the stable ^{12}C, which is the daughter product, exists at the beginning. This is impossible to determine. (2) Decay rate has been constant, that is, its half-life has been constant. This second assumption does not take into account numerous factors such as heat, radiation, solar flares, etc. that can speed up the decay rate. (3) It is in a closed system with no outside influences. A closed system is a theoretical situation where there would be nothing to influence the decay rate.

Over 150 years ago (long before radiometric dating came into being), evolutionary geologists determined the geologic ages of the rocks according to the fossils contained within them in order to show the evolutionary bias. The fossils were dated by their supposed evolutionary position and so dated the rocks: a tautology. There was no actual reference to time or any dating technique. The only criteria was to show the "evolution" of animals from lower to higher order. Even with radiometric dating, there is no consistency in dates given to many samples.

When I was working in Denver and needed a rock sample age-dated, I would send it to a laboratory. The technician would always ask, "Where did it come from, and how old do you think it is?" It didn't bother me at the time, but now I know that they can't really rely on their dating procedure and need to have some idea of what the geologist expects the date to be. They get such a wide range of dates that they will pick the one that comes out closest to the expected date.

What is a half-life of a radiometric isotope? A radiometric isotope is an unstable substance that gives off an alpha particle (a helium nucleus) and becomes something else; for example, ^{238}Uranium is unstable and goes through a series of other isotopes until it becomes ^{206}Lead, which is stable. A half-life is the time it takes for half of the unstable substance to change. For instance, the half-life of ^{218}Polonium is three minutes. If I start with a pound of ^{218}Polonium, in three minutes I will have half a pound of ^{218}Polonium and half a pound of something else. In the next three minutes, I will have one-quarter pound of ^{218}Polonium and three-quarters of a pound of something else.

At the fifth International Conference on Creationism in 2003, Dr. John Baumgardner of the Institute for Creation Research presented his new ^{14}Carbon findings. Advanced technology has resulted in extremely precise measurements of the ratio of ^{14}C to ^{12}C in extremely small samples. They found ^{14}C in samples of fossil-bearing rock that should have *no* ^{14}C in remaining them at all, and therefore become a huge anomaly to uniformitarian scientists (Morris 2003).

Dr. John Baumgardner presented his exciting results of measurable concentrations of ^{14}C in fossilized organics like coal. Using a new method of Atomic Mass Spectrometry, coal is found to average about one quarter of one percent of modern levels of ^{14}C. Coal which is dated to be on the order of 100 million years old by conventional dating methods should contain none. This is strong evidence for a young earth (Morris 2003).

At the same conference, Dr. Russell Humphreys presented a new estimated date for Noah's Flood based on the Helium content of zircons in granite.

"The Helium content of zircons embedded in granite is due to the radioactive decay of Uranium. The decay rate of Uranium appears to have been accelerated in the recent past violating the assumptions of conventional dating methods" (Morris 2003).

The Young Island That Looks Old — Uniformitarian thinking expects that long, slow, gradual processes are required to produce geological formations. However, the island of Surtsey, off the coast of Iceland, was formed in only a few days in 1963. An undersea volcanic eruption catastrophically created the island, but surprisingly to geologists, it contains features with signs of great age. Even the local geologist, Sigurdur Thoarinsson, was amazed. "On Surtsey, only a few months sufficed for a landscape to be created which was so varied and mature that it was almost beyond belief" (Wieland 1995). This amazing island not only has a lava dome and flows, but sandy beaches, craggy cliffs, gravel banks, and lagoons. "There were hollows, glens, and soft undulating land. There were fractures and faultscarps, . . . lava cliffs, . . . boulders worn by the surf, some of which were almost round" (Wieland 1995). The mature features of this island fly in the face of the evolutionary dating scheme.

Rocks from Recent Volcanic Eruption Dated Old — Some rocks from a volcanic eruption that was documented to have occurred 170 years ago were sampled. The lab that used radiometric dating techniques to determine the age of these samples misdated the rocks to be anywhere from 160 million to three billion years old. This is far beyond a normal margin of error.

Fresh Tree Roots Fossilized — A section of forest in Canada was being clear-cut to install power lines. Tree roots left in the clear-cut area were "fossilized" by intense heat from an electrical charge when the power line fell to the ground over the weekend. Samples of these tree roots that looked fossilized were taken to a lab for age analysis. Technicians at the lab were informed of the circumstances of the tree roots that had been living the week before. They said the samples would date millions of years old due to the heat applied to them, because heat throws off the results. These same scientists routinely date volcanic rocks this same way, and they certainly get very hot.

Skull 1470 — Evolutionists greeted with tremendous excitement the unearthing of a skull in Kenya that was labeled Skull 1470. Found in 1972 by paleoanthropologist, Richard Leakey and initially reconstructed by him, the skull was believed to be the link between australopithiecines (which means "southern apes") and *Homo erectus*. This initial reconstruction gave the skull some human-like traits, including a flat face and no pronounced brow ridge. Even some creationists were left wondering about a supposed "missing link." It did not take long, however, for other scientists to voice their doubts about this find. The age of 1.9 million years, which was determined by radiometric dating, was much too old to fit into the pre-established evolutionary scale for hominids. Subsequent reconstructions between 1977 and 1992 showed much more ape-like characteristics. Christopher Hummer, a Creationist, pointed out a number of ape-like traits in the skull in 1977: occipital flaring, long upper lip, cranio-facial ratio indicative of australopethecine. This became very significant. Later reconstructions, which took advantage of the study of growth lines, showed a much more ape-like jaw and cranial structure. It now appears that Skull 1470 does not fit into the evolutionary scenario (Mehlert 1999).

Alpha Particles in the Atmosphere — Dr. Larry Vardiman has done research on the accumulation of alpha particles in the atmosphere. An alpha particle is a nucleus of Helium from which the electron has been stripped away, leaving only a proton. Alpha particles are given off as a radioactive isotope decays. These alpha particles do not dissipate into space, but rather it has been discovered that the sun is adding more to the atmosphere. There is only enough accumulation of alpha particles in our atmosphere to account for a few thousand years (Bliss 1988).

Radiohalos As Evidence That the Earth is Young — Robert Gentry has been doing research in radiometric dating for thirty years and is a Biblical creationist. His work with Polonium halos is one of the most compelling evidences for sudden, recent creation. Radiohalos are formed as an unstable isotope gives off an alpha particle and a burst of energy. The burst of energy discolors the surrounding rock, leaving the characteristic halo. Radiohalos are very specific in their rings and can be used like fingerprints to identify various isotopes. Gentry has found radiohalos in a coal deposit in Colorado where the Uranium–to-Lead ratios indicate that the formation is only a few thousand years old. These radiohalos are in the early stage of development and raise important questions about the supposed geologic age of the formation (Ackerman 1993).

Gentry has found Polonium halos in all types of rocks: granites, quartz, diamonds, biotite, coal, etc. Polonium isotopes, found in the decay series of Uranium, are very unstable. ^{218}Polonium has a half-life of three minutes, ^{214}Polonium has a half-life of 164 microseconds (that means it doesn't hang around very long), and ^{210}Polonium has a half-life of 138.4 days. What is so amazing is that Polonium halos are found in granite, the basement rocks of the earth, with no Uranium present. If the rocks were very old and had cooled over long periods of time, then we should not be able to see Polonium halos. Since they have such very short half-lives, they would have given off their radiation energy long before the molten rock cooled. The rock has to be solid in order to have an energy halo recorded in it. Therefore, in order for Polonium halos to be present in rocks where there is no Uranium present, the rock had to have been created in its solid form with the Polonium in it simultaneously. This is fantastic and indisputable evidence for sudden, recent creation (Gentry 1995).

Over-Pressured Zones in Oil Reservoirs — Oil well fluid pressures, the kind that produce the gushers you see in old movies, would have dissipated if the earth were very old. To form a reservoir rock, a porous rock layer needs to be capped off with a layer of impermeable rock. A statistical study of oil well reservoir pressures shows that even in highly over-pressured zones, the pressure dissipates over time. Even conservative calculations indicate that highly over-pressured zones would reach equilibrium with the surrounding area in about 10,000 years. Therefore, when oil wells encounter over-pressured zones it means that the reservoir has to be less than 10,000 years old. A friend of mine was sitting a well in Louisiana when it hit an over-pressured zone. Ten thousand feet of drill pipe was thrown up out of the hole like it was spaghetti, killing several of the crew. That much pressure still in the reservoir would indicate that it was young.

Oil itself does not need millions of years to form. It can be produced in a laboratory in a matter of weeks. Right now oil is forming off the coast of California in an area known as the Guaymas Basin. This oil is forming near a geothermal vent and is bubbling to the surface. All it takes to make oil is the right amounts of temperature and pressure and the right ingredients, not millions of years.

Fast Diamonds — Presently there are techniques for manufacturing artificial diamonds in only a few months. By exposing carbon to heat and pressure, the new artificial diamonds are being created for commercial use. The following quotation is from an article in *Creation* magazine: "Now researchers can transform graphite into 'ultrahard' pure diamonds in only a few minutes under static high pressure and temperatures of 2,300 – 2,500°C. With their extreme hardness (being polycrystaline, they are even harder than single-crystal diamonds), these transparent artificial diamonds could be used in industry where real diamonds are currently used to cut and polish other hard materials" (*Creation* 2003).

Erosion — If erosion has been going on for millions of years at the present rate according to the theory of uniformitarianism, then the ocean basins should be full of sediment. There is only enough to account for a few thousand years of accumulation. Also, the continents would be worn down to sea level at the same rate of erosion in just fourteen million years.

Stalactites and Stalagmites Can Form Rapidly — Stalactites and stalagmites do not, as commonly believed, take millions of years to form from dissolved minerals in water that dripped slowly over long ages of time. In some old buildings, such as the Lincoln Monument in Washington D.C., there are stalactites over five feet long that have formed in less than fitfy years! In one cave there is a bat encased in mineral, lying on a stalactite. This poor bat, whose outline of head and wings is clearly visible, did not have time to decay before being encased in the mineral. Therefore, the mineral deposit did not take very long to form.

Rate of Coral Reef Growth — Coral reefs are made by the animals in them that build up the calcium carbonate material—their skeleton—that is their home. Until coral growth rates were actually observed and measured, it was believed that they were very slow. In 1997 a group of scientists built laser devices to measure the rate of coral growth. The growth rate of 1.25 inches to 2.5 inches per year which they measured indicates the age of the earth as less than 10,000 years, which fits the Creation model (Vago et al 1997).

Erosion at Niagara Falls — The rate of erosion occurring at Niagara Falls is a known rate. The place where the Falls originated is also known. The combination of these two known factors indicates that Niagara Falls was at its place of origin about 5,000 years ago. This means that the Falls have eroded to their present location in only 5,000 years. This is another problem for evolutionists, but it fits nicely with the Creation model.

Sea Salinity — The salinity of the sea and the amount of dissolved minerals in it indicate a young age for the oceans, probably around 5,000 years. All the world's rivers carry these substances into the sea every day. If the earth were millions of years old, then there should be much more mineral content and salt content in the oceans. Evolutionists cannot explain where millions of years' worth of salt went. But if it is considered that the present oceans have been accumulating salt and minerals only since the Flood, then there is no problem, because there is no missing salt (Austin & Humphreys 1991).

Crustal Build-Up — Build-up of the Earth's crust occurs in several ways, including volcanic activity. The rate at which volcanic activity adds material to the Earth's crust is known. The rate of crustal build-up from volcanic activity alone indicates that the earth is quite young.

Considering only this one source for crustal material, the present volume of material would have accumulated in a few thousand years.

The Sun — The source of the sun's energy is being debated. Over ten years and millions of dollars have been spent unsuccessfully trying to prove that the energy source is a thermonuclear reaction. It was postulated 150 years ago that gravitational collapse was the source of the sun's energy. There is some evidence to indicate that the sun's diameter is shrinking at the rate of one percent every one thousand years. Going back twenty million years would place the sun's diameter out to where the Earth is now. Even 100,000 years ago life on the earth would have been impossible. If, however, the earth is only 6,000 years old, then the sun would have been only six percent larger, and the temperature would have been slightly warmer, which again fits the Creation model (Akridge 1980).

Secular scientists argue that even a slightly larger sun would not have allowed for historically documented total solar eclipses. They misrepresent Creationist views in their challenges to solar shrinkage. A skeptic's reply to Creationist views misleadingly gives the impression that F.R. Stephenson, in his paper on historical eclipses, is discussing the total eclipse of July 17, 709 B.C. Andrew Snelling clarifies the misinterpretation:

> The impression left with the reader is that Stephenson on p. 161 of his 1982 paper on "Historical Eclipses" discusses the total eclipse of July 17, 709 B.C. Nothing could be further from the truth. Nowhere on p.161 does Stephenson even mention the July 17, 709 B.C. total eclipse, and when he does talk about a rate of shrinkage of about 0.16 second of arc per century Stephenson only derives that conclusion from the "six total solar eclipses from AD 1715 to 1925" as well as the observed duration of 30 transits of Mercury. Stephenson only mentions the July 17, 709 B.C. total eclipse once in his whole paper, and that is in a table on p.157 where no mention is made of any comparison of the sun's size between then and now. . . . It is wrong for [the authors] to say that there is no solid evidence of shrinkage or that this is "essentially a null result." The calculated shrinkage rate is **not** no shrinkage (Snelling 1989).

There is definitely solid evidence for a small rate of shrinkage, and the Creationist's shrinkage rate fits in with the Creation model of the origin of the universe. The rate of shrinkage calculated by Stephenson of only 0.02 second of arc per century, which is extremely small, is still a problem for evolutionists, because at that rate the sun would have been too large for any life to exist on the earth only 100 million years ago, much too short for evolution.

The Moon — The moon was created by God on the fourth day of the Creation week. God called for lights to be in the sky, to separate day from night, and to mark the seasons, days, and years. God made two great lights, the lesser light to rule the night. Astronomers have measured that the moon is moving away from the earth at about 1.5 inches per year. This means that 1.37 billion years ago it would have been touching the earth. If it had started out any distance away from the earth it would have been out of sight in the supposed 4.5 billion years of evolutionary time. The moon could have never been any closer than 11,500 miles, known as the Roche Limit, due to the gravitational forces that would have torn it apart (Sarfati 1998). Scientists admit that they do not know where the moon came from, so how can they speak so matter-of-factly about the origin of our earth and our universe?

Comets — Evolutionary theory says that our solar system is 5 billion years old. As comets pass by our sun, the power emitted from the sun (photons) partially disintegrates the comets. The beautiful tail of the comet that we see is that part that is being blown away. Therefore, the comets will eventually disintegrate completely in about 100,000 years. The measured rate of comet disintegration has forced scientists to realize that all short-term comets would be gone in 10,000 years. It has been estimated that we have five million short-term comets still orbiting our solar system, yet another great indication that the universe is young (Steidl 1983). Evolutionist astronomers have a hard time with this enigma, so a man named Jan Oort came up with a theory that there is a *nest* of comets out there somewhere that periodically shakes lose some comets that then enter our solar system. This "nest" can't be seen or detected, but it must be there. It sounds like the story of "The Emperor's New Clothes." They are relying on man's wisdom, which is foolishness to God.

V. The Big Bang Theory

The Big Bang theory imagines that all the matter in the universe was once condensed into an infinitely small dot that contained an infinite amount of mass and energy. This dot exploded (no explanation for the cause of the explosion is ever given) and the explosion formed all the chemical elements. By some unknown process, protons and neutrons were able to come together to form nuclei, and then by some other unknown process, these new nuclei were able to combine with the appropriate number of elections. This explosion threw matter out into space for millions and billions of years. At some point, gravity supposedly became an effective force (no explanation is given as to why particles of matter would start to attract together rather than continue to expand outward into space) and matter then began to clump into primordial swirling gases. These clouds of swirling gases formed the first protogalaxies, which were cold and dark and without stars. From these *cold* protogalaxies came the galaxies: clusters of stars which are *very hot*, burning stellar objects. It is of interest to note that not all scientists agree with the Big Bang theory, and many have never agreed with it at all.

What Causes the "Red Shift"? — An astronomer named Edwin Hubble in the 1920s found what he believed were distant stars that had their light waves lengthened, or shifted to the red end of the spectrum. This is what is called the red shift. In *Compton's Interactive Encyclopedia*, F. Wagner Schlesinger states:

> The Red Shift of the stars, which astronomers say indicates that the stars are moving away from us, is actually due to the fact that they are so massive that their gravitational attraction is "dragging back" or slowing down their own light (slowing down or lengthening of light waves shifts them toward the red end of the spectrum), thus giving a false indication, interpreted by astronomers as the stars moving away (*Compton's Interactive Encyclopedia*, s.v. "Relativity").

The red shift can be compared to the Doppler Effect that is heard when a person is standing on a street corner as an ambulance passes by. The sound waves from the siren on the ambulance are compressed (shortened) as the ambulance approaches the person. At the moment the ambulance siren is even with the person, the observer would hear the siren with the same sound wave as the people in the ambulance. Then as the ambulance passes the person on the corner, the sound waves are elongated (lengthened) because the source of the sound is moving away from the observer. Therefore, according to Schlesinger, the red shift seen in the stars does not necessarily mean that they are moving away (thus indicating that the universe is expanding) but rather that they are so massive that their own gravitational pull slows down the light as it escapes from them.

A secular website contains an article by J. T. Wong that enumerates several aspects of the universe that cannot be explained by using the Big Bang theory:

1. It does not explain where the singularity and the start of the universe's expansion

was located. 2. It also does not explain how the immense amount of matter and radiation in the universe originated. 3. The expansion of the gases in the big bang theory should have made the universe completely homogeneous. However, galaxies and large scale structures produce "walls" which fence off areas of little, or no space structures. Even analysis of the background radiation suggests that the universe was pockmarked with relatively empty areas, long before galaxies and stars formed. 4. Finally, all the theories and laws of physics used to describe the universe as it is today, break down when attempting to explain the behaviour of the singularity. This implies that science can deal with everything that occurred after the big bang, but not before or during the actual big bang (Wong, retrieved 2003).

Why Does the Universe Hold Together? — Scientists cannot explain the gravitational attraction of the galaxies, which should have dissipated or moved apart over supposed eons of time because there is not enough mass to hold them together and they are constantly in motion. This would be analogous to a bunch of helium-filled balloons held down under a huge net. The moment the net was removed and the balloons released, they would begin to move away from each other. The more time that elapsed from the moment the net was removed, the farther apart the balloons would move. An interesting observation in our universe is that the galaxies are grouped together in clusters. There has never been a single field galaxy observed; they are always in clusters. Going back to the balloon analogy, this would mean that the net had just recently been removed. This is another good indication that the universe is young. God's Word gives us a good explanation for why the universe behaves this way in Heb. 1:3, which says, "He sustains all things by His powerful Word." God's Word is not good enough for many scientists, so they have come up with the term "Cold Dark Matter," which they say makes up 99% of the universe. This cold dark matter cannot be measured or even detected. Most astronomers believe that it is this invisible, undetectable mass that holds the universe together (Wieland 1996). Which one is easier to believe in: the invisible, hypothetical something that is supposed to be out there, or the Word of God?

Where Did The Initial Energy Come From? — Astronomers who have become famous with the Big Bang Theory believe that the universe started from nothing and then exploded. Well, at least they got the first part right. But they offer no explanation of where the matter came from to form everything in the universe or where the energy came from for the bang. Even these astronomers know that one of the most fundamental laws of physics is that energy cannot be created or destroyed. (See Section VI below.) John Maddox wrote in the lead editorial in *Nature*: "Apart from being philosophically unacceptable, the Big Bang is an over-simple view of how the Universe began, and it is unlikely to survive the decade ahead" (Maddox 1989). Another admission of truth.

Time **Magazine Article** — The cover story for the March 6, 1995 issue of *Time* magazine was "When Did the Universe Begin?" The new information which astronomers have been analyzing since the Hubble telescope had its vision repaired has left them in a state of chaos and constantly arguing with each other over the age of the universe. One analysis says that the universe is not expanding but rather is moving toward the constellation Virgo. Other astronomers want to throw this information out because it doesn't fit with their cosmological theories; even though they cannot prove the analysis to be incorrect, they insist that it must be incorrect.

According to the article, many astronomers are angry at their fellow scientists who say that the universe is now only eight billion years old, as they hold tenaciously to the twenty-billion-year age of the universe. There is a great gulf between theory and observation as each scientist plugs his pet theory into a computer with his pet parameters and has his desired results printed out. If the universe is only eight billion years old, then what is to be done about the stars that have been assigned ages much older than the universe itself? An article in *Time* magazine explains:

In fairness, it must be acknowledged that cosmologists have had very little information to go on, at least until very recently. The distant galaxies that bear witness to the universe's origin, evolution and structure are excruciatingly faint, and it takes every bit of skill observers have to tease out their secrets. In a very real sense, cosmology has only lately crossed the dividing line from theology into true science. The experts don't know for sure how old or how big the universe is. They don't know what most of it is made of. They don't know in any detail how it began or how it will end. And, beyond the local cosmic neighborhood, they don't know much about what it looks like (Lemonick and Nash 1995).

In other words, they don't know much about anything in the universe, yet they are professing theories of its origin to the public as though they are facts. In actuality, the newly acquired data doesn't match their own hypothesis, and astronomers have no explanations.

How Could An Accretion Disk Form? — Let us suppose for a moment that we did start from a big bang. Electrons and protons and neutrons come together in just the right proportions to make all the various elements, and matter starts zooming out across the universe. The favorite theory of how our solar system came to be is that it formed from an accretion disk when clumps of matter started to swirl around in a flattened disk shape. My first observation is that it would be difficult for matter that is moving in a straight line away from some explosion to start swirling around together. But for the sake of argument, we will say that it did. Now there is a disk of material swirling around in space that will become our solar system. According to the Law of the Conservation of Angular Momentum, everything in our solar system should be spinning in the same direction. This law states that for any spinning (or rotating) object, when pieces fly off it, they will continue to spin in the same direction. For example, if you had a merry-go-round full of kids and you sped up the merry-go-round faster and faster until kids started flying off, the children would rotate in the same direction as the merry-go-round. What is observed in our solar system is that the Sun spins clockwise and the planets move counter-clockwise. Venus and Neptune rotate backwards. Of the sixty moons in our solar system, eleven rotate backwards and four travel backwards. Two planets even have moons traveling in both directions. This is very hard on the accretion disk theory and the Big Bang theory which we will now call the big OOPS! I think God made our solar system this way just to make the Big Bang theory look ridiculous. An article in the March1995 *Discover* magazine states: "The field (of cosmology) is in a troubled state, a disconcerting or an exciting one, depending on your personality—a state in which even the most basic assumptions seem open to question" (Flamsteed 1995). Even evolutionary scientists are beginning to understand they have major problems.

VI. Thermodynamics

The First Law of Thermodynamics — The First Law of Thermodynamics is also called the Law of Conservation of Energy. It states that energy is neither created nor destroyed, but can be changed from one form to another. God used His creative powers during the

Creation Week to make everything there is out of nothing, and this first law probably became effective at the end of Creation.

The Second Law of Thermodynamics — The Second Law of Thermodynamics is that energy tends to even out all over the universe. No work can be done when energy is evened out and reaches equilibrium. This process is known as entropy. Energy is defined as always moving toward a more disorganized state. Heat, by itself, always flows from high temperature to low temperature and spreads out evenly in all directions. This means that hot things cool down; cold things warm up; metal rusts; things decay; complex things become simple. Nothing in the observable universe is becoming more complicated. The increase in order and complexity required by evolution violates this Second Law. Since God created everything perfectly in the Garden of Eden and He was present there, all things would have maintained perfection. Perfection ended when sin entered and the Second Law came into effect at that point.

Dr. Henry Morris of the Institute for Creation Research made the following observation about the universal principle of the Second Law of Thermodynamics (also know as the law of increasing entropy):

> The very existence of the law of entropy points to a Creator, because systems that are wearing out must first have been made new, and beings that die must first have been given life. The very idea of a universal naturalistic evolution of all things into more complex systems is contrary to all real scientific data and is contradicted by all human experience (Morris 2003).

VII. Problems with Darwinian Theory

Changes over Time — Charles Darwin believed that living things became more complex in evolutionary steps due to beneficial changes over millions of years. These changes were supposed to be passed on to the next generation. (Darwin did not know what a mutation was, as DNA had not yet been discovered.) Small changes known as microevolution do occur within a species due to the genetic variability God has programmed into living things. But we don't find macroevolution, or one species becoming another species, occurring. No macroevolutionary steps are observed in nature or are ever seen in the fossil record. This means that no new genetic information has been input that would change one creature into another creature. What we see instead is a loss of genetic information.

Changes Must Be Beneficial (Or At Least Neutral) — Each change in an organism, according to Darwin, must be beneficial to the organism in order to be maintained and passed along to the offspring. How would a small portion of an eye be beneficial to a worm? Or a small piece of a wing beneficial to a fish? Nearly all mutations are harmful, or at the very least neutral, to the creature and most often result in its death. This is not improvement. Can you imagine the first bird that decided that it wanted to become a woodpecker? It would bang its head on a tree, it's beak would fold up, and since it did not have the sufficient brain padding of a woodpecker, it would knock itself out, fall to the forest floor, be eaten by the nearest predator, and never pass on its desire to become a woodpecker (Juhasz 1996).

Dogs Are Still Dogs — Dogs have been bred for specific characteristics since the time of the Egyptians. In all those years of genetic manipulation, the result has never been anything other than a dog. Genetically dogs are still dogs—everything from the smallest Chihuahua to the largest Newfoundland. This is variation within a kind and does not conflict with Scripture, because God built genetic variation into all kinds. Note that "kind" does not equate to "species." "Kinds" in the Bible meant dog kind or cat kind or elephant kind—not species. Species distinctions were not made until modern scientific technology was available.

No Viable Offspring — A mule is a sterile hybrid between a horse and a donkey, which means that it is not capable of reproducing itself. Horses and donkeys have both existed in the wild since Creation, but wild mules are not found with them in nature because the horses and donkeys would not normally mate. Man's intervention with breeding techniques has resulted in the mule. But even man's intervention cannot make a mule capable of reproducing iteself.

VIII. DNA and Protein

Structure of DNA Molecules — DNA stands for deoxyribonucleic acid. All biological molecules are either left-handed or right-handed in their structural orientation. Living organisms use *only* left-handed molecules in their DNA. Therefore, all protein chains must be 100% left-handed for life to function. For sugars to be useful and to combine with the proteins, they must be configured in chains that are 100% right-handed, which doubly complicates the problem. This is not likely to happen by chance. However, if left to chance, their chemical reactions to each other would scramble any codes, not produce more complex codes (no input of new information). In other words, they would cancel each other out. The famous Stanley Miller experiment produced some amino acids, but they were a mix of 50% left-handed and 50% right-handed molecules, not capable of producing life (Wieland 1993).

Which Came First: DNA or Protein? — DNA is the code for making proteins, and proteins are the building blocks of life. DNA itself is made of protein so this becomes a chicken-and-egg conundrum: which came first? Proteins are made by way of the DNA code; DNA is made by using proteins (enzymes). A secular scientist reveals the seriousness of the problem:

> [The] interdependence between nucleic acids and proteins gives rise to what has been called the "chicken and egg" problem: in evolutionary terms, which of the two came first, or could they have evolved together? From the early days of the debate there have been disagreements. . . . Even today, the answer is by no means obvious (Palmer 1999).

Evolutionists have a problem with which came first. The answer is obvious to the Creationists, who have no problem with which came first, because God created with the ability to produce the egg. Other scientists working in the field of genetics reveal their problem with understanding the origins of proteins and DNA:

> It remains a mystery how the undirected process of mutation, combined with natural selection [hear the word "evolution"] has resulted in the creation [Did they say creation?] of thousands of new proteins with extraordinarily diverse and well-optimized functions. This problem is particularly acute for tightly integrated molecular systems that consist of many interacting parts. In these systems it is not clear how a new function for any protein might be selected for unless the other members of the complex are already present, creating a molecular version of the ancient evolutionary riddle of the chicken and the egg (Thorton & DeSalle, 2000).

A scientist friend, Frank Sherwin, says this is one of his favorite quotes from the atheist Francis Crick, who in the 1950s helped describe the double helix structure of DNA: "Biologists must constantly keep in mind that what they see was not designed, but rather evolved" (Crick 1988).

Combination of DNA — The possible combinations of human DNA are ten to the eighty-seventh power (10^{87}). That is 1,000,000,000,000,000,000,000,000,000,000,000,000,000, 000,000,000,000,000,000,000,000,000,000,000,000,000,000. The number of seconds in 4.5 billion years (the time for presumed evolution) is ten to the twenty-fifth power (10^{25}). That is 10,000,000,000,000,000,000,000,000. As you look at these numbers carefully you can see that 10^{25} is really very tiny number compared to 10^{87}. In fact, it is smaller by a factor of 10^{62}. If you subtract 10^{25} from 10^{87} power you essentially still have 10^{87}. (Take 10^{6} or 1,000,000 and subtract 10^{3} or 1,000 and you still have about a million.) As you can see, random chance, i.e. evolution, would have to get very lucky to get it right (properly combine the

DNA molecule) after so few of the possible combinations were tried. One chance out of 10^62 is essentially zero. It is one chance in 100,000,000,000,000,000,000,000,000,000,000,000, 000,000,000,000,000,000,000,000. So what mathematics tells us is that basically random chance has NO chance. Chandra Wickramasinghe, the mathematician who assisted Sir Fred Hoyle with his DNA research, explained on www.space.com, "It is mathematically impossible for life to have evolved on Earth. . . . The emergence of life from a primordial soup on the Earth is merely an article of faith that scientists are finding difficult to shed. There is no experimental evidence to support this at the present time (Matthews 2003).

IX. Ernst Haeckel

The Deliberate Lie — In 1866 Ernst Haeckel was determined to prove the newly popular Darwinian theory of evolution, so he deliberately falsified drawings of a human embryo to show a resemblance to other embryos of fish, salamander, turtle, rabbit, dog, chicken, etc. He used this false evidence to "prove" his theory that "Ontogeny recapitulates phylogeny"—which means that the embryonic cycle of a creature depicts the evolutionary history of that species. Haeckel altered drawings by other scientists to prove his point. These altered drawings were proven to be fraudulent by one of his own colleagues, Professor Wilhelm His, Sr., in 1874. Haeckel tried to blame his draftsman for the alterations, but he himself was the draftsman (Grigg 1998). However, I was still being taught Haeckel's theory as a fact in college in 1972! You can see the great lengths to which evolutionists will go to try to "prove" their old disproven theories since they have no new valid ones to cling to.

Gill Slits — In his attempt to show our "fish phase" of evolution, Haeckel called the pharyngeal pouches gill slits. What he called gill slits, however, have nothing to do with respiration. The pharyngeal pouches of the embryo develop into the middle ear canal, the parathyroid gland, and the thymus gland (Grigg 1996).

Yolk Sac — To show our "bird phase," Haeckel falsely labeled the blood-cell-forming pouch as a yolk sac. A chicken embryo is nourished by the yolk sac, while a human baby is nourished in the mother's womb. The so-called yolk sac, as Haeckel labeled it, on the baby's body forms his first blood cells. This doesn't have anything to do with nourishing the developing baby (Grigg 1996).

Tail Bone — In order to show our "monkey phase," Haeckel exaggerated the length of the developing coccyx. The last bone—actually four fused bones—in the spine is the coccyx, deliberately misnamed the "tail bone" by Haeckel. It sticks out in a developing baby because its appearance stimulates the growth of the legs. It is also the point of attachment for the muscles that allow humans to sit upright. We never had a tail (Grigg, 1996). When I broke my coccyx I found out how important this bone is!

X. Human Senses — Marvelous Design, Incredible Sensitivity

(See *Creation Anatomy: A Study Guide to the Miracles of the Human Body.*)

Ear — The complexities of transferring sound wave energy into electrical impulses to the brain that are received as hearing are enormous. As sound energy enters the ear canal, it is changed into mechanical energy by the bones of the middle ear. This mechanical energy causes a pressure wave in the perilymph fluid within the cochlea, which moves against the basilar membrane, on which 16,000 hair cells in each ear are located. The hair cells then vibrate, and on top of them are tiny stereocilia which then brush against the tectorial membrane, which converts these mechanical impulses into electrical energy that the brain interprets as sound. Nothing that intricate and complicated could have happened by chance.

Eye — The receptors in our eyes are only part of the process of vision. The brain has to weave together bits of information about motion, form, depth, and color for us to see. The pieces of the picture are interpreted by a complex network of processing centers. The brain takes signals from the retinas and relays them through the lateral geniculate bodies, and then passes them to areas in the back of the brain. Other areas of the brain are involved which are yet unidentified. Darwin himself said, "To suppose that the eye with all its inimitable contrivances for adjusting focus to different distances, for admitting different amounts of light, and for the correction of spherical and chromatic aberration, could have been formed by natural selection, seems, I freely confess, absurd in the highest degree" (Darwin 1859, chapter 6). A correct observation.

Smell and Taste — The chemical receptors on our tongue sense four basic things (sweet, sour, salty, and bitter), but provide us an incredible variety of flavors. The nose enhances our ability to taste. Taste is actually a combination of taste and smell. Molecules of food are drawn up to the olfactory neurons in the nose. Taste buds on the tongue relay their messages to the brain along with the olfactory bulbs, which send signals to the brain for interpretation.

Touch — Touch involves very complex neural circuitry. Nerves all over the body send signals to the brain. This allows us the sensory range from touching soft baby skin to having a thumb smashed with a hammer. The entire surface of our skin is a sensory organ. It is so sensitive that a person can feel when a tiny ant is crawling on his arm or leg. Sensory nerves are concentrated on the tips of the fingers to give us incredible tactile sensation and ability to manipulate even very tiny objects.

XI. The Fossil Record

No Transitional Fossils — Transitional fossils, if they existed, would be fossils of animals evolving from a lower form to a higher form. They would be very important evidence for the macroevolution of animals. However, the fossil record shows no evidence of any transitional fossils. If evolution were a fact and things have been evolving for eons of time, there should be large numbers of transitional fossils. A museum in Germany has a collection of over 200,000 fossils of plants and animals that are identical to living forms today. Cockroaches that are supposed to be 350 million years old are identical to cockroaches today. Why have they not shown any evolution in all that alleged "evolutionary" time?

Stasis and Extinction — Stasis and extinction are the only two things that do show up in the fossil record. Either the organisms have stayed the same (stasis) over millions and millions of years, or they disappeared from the fossil record altogether (extinction). The plant Metasequoia, thought to be extinct 100 million years ago, has been found growing in China. The Coelacanth, a fish thought to be 100 million years old, has been caught by the dozens off the coast of Madagascar since 1938! Stories and legends abound of a Plesiosaur-like creature living in Loch Ness and Lake Champlain.

No Evidence of Invertebrate Changing to Vertebrate — There is no evidence of any invertebrate becoming a vertebrate. There is no transition from a jellyfish to a completely vertebrate fish. There is no transition from a fish to a land animal, or bird to reptile. Archaeopteryx was thought to be transitional but is now considered a true bird. It has feathers and bones like a true bird. Also, there are three species of birds today that have claws on their wings. A fossil found in China was supposed to show a dinosaur with feathers on its neck. Evolutionists

32

jumped on this as evidence of a transitional fossil. However, it was difficult to tell what the half-centimeter objects were. A paleontologist from the University of Kansas says, "We generally get more hard evidence with alien abductions than we have here" (Wieland 1994). This is a great way of saying that they don't have any evidence.

Evolutionists claim that only the most so-called primitive animals were living in the Cambrian age, the oldest sedimentary rocks. But it has now been discovered that all types of animals, including vertebrate fish, are represented in the oldest sedimentary rocks. And none of them show any previous transitional forms. In his review of Jeffrey Levington's book *Genetics, Paleontology and Macroevolution*, Peter Forey writes concerning the lack of evidence of fossils in the Precambrian rocks:

> Although the Precambrian metazoan fossil record is poor, it is not mute; and almost certainly the lack of skeletonised animals is a real phenomenon. Molecular evidence, although fraught with difficulties of interpretation, points to the existence of metazoans well before the base of the Cambrian (Forey 2003).

If the evidence is fraught with difficulties of interpretation, how can these scientists come up with such concrete analysis? This scientist is even surprised at the lack of evidence of skeletonised animals. In the conclusion of his review, Forey writes, "Do not expect answers. Rather, the strength of this book lies in stimulating thought" (Forey 2003). It sounds like the evolutionists do not have a great deal of answers.

No Physical Evidence for Macroevolution — There is no evidence of macroevolution occurring in the past or in the present. Microevolution does occur within the variability of a species, but macroevolution has not been observed. If evolution had occurred or was occurring at present, then it would impossible for us to identify any living creature because they would constantly be in transition from one form to another. And if you think the evidence for animal evolution is scarce, the evidence for plant evolution is almost nonexistent.

The Peppered Moth — Scientists used to point to the peppered moth as an example of modern evolution. The moths changed from predominately white to predominately black during the Industrial Revolution. Prior to the Industrial Revolution, the bark of trees and the sides of buildings were light colored. More black moths were eaten by birds because they were easily seen against the light color. After belching smokestacks covered the trees and building with soot, more of the white moths were eaten by the birds because they now stood out against the blackened trees and buildings, and the black moths became predominant. This is now recognized as an example of genetic variation within a species (sometimes called microevolution), not macroevolution, where one species changes to another species.

Supposed Horse Ancestry — *Eohippus,* the alleged ancestor to the modern horse, and *Equus*, the modern horse, have been found together in the same strata. Therefore *Eohippus* could not have been an ancestor. The so-called pre-dawn horse has now been identified as a type of hyrax similar to that living in Africa and Asia and is more related to a rabbit than a horse. Yet the horse evolution chain is still found in many prominent museums today.

Living Fossils — There are numerous examples, numbering in the thousands, of fossilized plants and animals that look identical to those seen today. Dr. Joachim Sheven has over 200,000 examples, including animals such as horseshoe crabs, shrimps, oysters, and insects; and plants such as the ginkgo, sassafras, bread fruit tree, palm tree, etc. (Wieland 1993). Dr. Sheven calls them living fossils because the living version looks identical to the fossilized version.

XII. Bad Science and Deliberate Hoaxes

Neanderthal Man — Neanderthal Man has long been included in the so-called ape-to-man chain. Due to much new scientific evidence, Neanderthal is now recognized as totally human. He was originally depicted with hair all over his body and walking hunched over. It is now known that the hunched back was due to arthritis and that Mr. Neanderthal was merely a genetic variation of the human species. The scientific name for Neanderthal man is even *Homo sapien neanderthalensis*! A *Time* magazine cover story on Neanderthal shows the new artist's conception of Mr. Neanderthal all cleaned up with no body hair, a shave, and a bald head. Quite a different interpretation of the same thing. A very interesting quote by L. A. Yaroch in *The Yearbook of Physical Anthropology* for 1996 states, "The uniqueness of Neanderthals appears to have been exaggerated." It is interesting to note how grudgingly this scientist admits that Neanderthal was one of us and not our ancestor. The human species has much variation as seen in the different races from the New York businessman to the Australian Aborigine. As an added thought, you can read what God thinks about prejudice and racism in Numbers 12:1-15. Miriam and Aaron were grumbling against Moses because he took a dark-skinned, Cushite woman for a wife, and Miriam was struck with leprosy.

Piltdown Man — Piltdown Man was a deliberate hoax. Two teachers took an ape jaw and filed down the teeth. The ape jaw was then put with a human cranium and stained to look old. These two men buried their "fossil" near the town of Piltdown, England, and waited for two years. They then took a class out to the site and had the students "discover" the "fossil." Piltdown Man gave evolutionists a boost and scared Christians into coming up with all kinds of theories to try to fit what the Bible says in with this new "science." We should never give up on God's Word just because some scientist makes a "great new discovery." Most of these new discoveries are really torn apart in the technical literature that laypeople don't usually read. God's Word will always prove to be true.

Lucy — "Lucy," found by Donald Johanson, was supposed to be one of our ancestors. Johanson claims the skeleton was 40% complete. However, other scientists assert that there is less material in Lucy than in many other skeletons that are 20% complete. Most of the bones are fragments. Other anthropologists who have examined the skeleton have said that the very incomplete skull was mostly "imagination" and the teeth are ape-like; most scientists conclude that Lucy was a form of orangutan, probably *Astralopithicus*. Johanson claimed he did *precise calculations* of the arm-to-leg ratio of Lucy to a value of 83.9%. In apes the arm and leg are about the same length, near 100%, whereas in humans the arm is 75% as long as the leg. That would put Lucy somewhere in between, which is a good place for a transitional form—except for the fact that Johanson admitted that he had *estimated* the length of the leg since it was broken and partially crushed. He used an estimate to come up with his very "precise" ratio. The ratio, therefore, is meaningless, because Johanson was only trying to make the evidence fit his preconceived idea. Very bad science.

Java Man — A Dutch doctor named Eugene DuBois was the first person to undertake a search specifically for fossils of human ancestors. He believed that humans and gibbons were closely related. In 1890, his workers found what he believed to be a human-like fossil of the right side of a lower jaw with three teeth. The next year they found a primate tooth and an intact skullcap that came to be known as Java Man. Then in 1892 they discovered a primate thigh bone 10-15 meters away from the Java Man skullcap. "In 1894 Dubois published a description of his fossils, naming them *Pithecanthropus erectus*, describing it as neither ape nor human, but something intermediate. Almost everyone agreed that the femur was effectively indistinguishable from a human femur, but it was widely doubted whether it had, as Dubois claimed, come from the same individual as the skullcap" (www.talkorigins.org/faqs/homs/edubois.html). The TalkOrigins website, which is very critical of Creationist arguments, does contain the following statement: "Creationists are right about one thing. Most modern scientists agree that the femur is more recent than the skullcap, belonging to a modern human. Some of the teeth found nearby are now thought to be from an orangutan, rather than *Homo erectus*" (www.talkorigins.org/faqs/homs/a_java/html). For excellent research and information on the Creation viewpoint please visit www.trueorigin.org.

A geologist at Berkeley Geochronology Center named Carl Swisher has re-evaluated the skulls found in Java. A *Newsweek* article from December 23, 1996, reports that Swisher tested the skulls several times, thinking he had made a mistake. Using the most advanced techniques, the skulls dated to only 27,000 years old. *Homo erectus* was supposed to have disappeared 250,000 years ago on the evolutionary scale. Swisher's tests meant that it was younger than anyone knew. Swisher even had to check to make certain the skulls were not *Homo sapiens*. These test results mean that modern man (*Homo sapiens*) and Neanderthal Man (now also called *Homo sapiens*) and Java Man (*Homo erectus*) were all contemporaneous. Swisher concludes, "It is no longer chronologically plausible to argue that *Homo sapiens* evolved from *Homo erectus*" (Kausman 1996). Visit the website www.talkorigins.org/gaqs/homs/a_java.html.

Nebraska Man — Nebraska Man was nothing more than a pig's tooth. Scientists used to believe that the type of pig that belonged to the tooth was extinct, but now we know that type of pig still exists. However, from this one tooth and a few artifacts, a whole "family" of our ape-like "ancestors" was drawn in great detail: the man, his wife and child, their animal skin garments, weapons, and food, all from a tooth! H. F. Osborn of the American Museum of Natural History in New York was convinced of Nebraska Man, and he was supported in England by Sir Grafton E. Smith of Manchester, an eminent anatomist. Every piece of evidence used for Nebraska Man has since been shown to be false, and he is no longer found in textbooks.

XIII. What Scientists Believe Is *Truth* Is Always Changing.

Frogs from Ponds — Scientists once believed that frogs were spontaneously generated from ponds. They observed that the frogs appeared seemingly out of nowhere. Spontaneous generation—the theory that life forms could spontaneously appear where there was no life before—was a common belief before good scientific methods were established.

Maggots from Meat — One man conducted an experiment to prove that maggots came from meat. He left meat outside, but he did not keep the flies away from it or provide a control set for the experiment; therefore, the experiment was flawed. An Italian scientist named Francesco Redi (1626-1697) devised a better experiment to test spontaneous generation in 1668. He placed a piece of meat in each of three jars. One jar was left open, one was covered with gauze, and one was sealed tightly. When flies landed on the meat in the open jar and laid eggs, maggots appeared. Flies also landed on the gauze and laid eggs there. But no flies got to the sealed meat, and therefore no maggots grew. Redi thus proved that spontaneous generation does not occur. His results, however, were not widely accepted in his time (www.kent.k12.wa.us/staff/rlynch/sci_class/chap01/redi.html). (See Francesco Redi experiment on page 124).

Flies and Rats from Garbage — A belief widely accepted by most townspeople of the Middle Ages was that piles of garbage generated flies and rats. They observed that there would be no flies and rats until they began to pile their garbage at the edge of town. Then flies and rats would appear. This again was the false assumption of spontaneous generation.

Recipe for Mice — A philosopher/chemist once believed he had found a recipe for growing mice when he left his sweaty shirt in a barn where some grain had fallen on it. In a few days he noticed that it was covered with mice. He repeated his "experiment" with the same results and concluded that they had come from the sweaty shirt and grain (PBS, *Recipe for Mice* 1994).

Spontaneous Generation —A French scientist, Louis Pasteur (1822-1895) validated earlier experiments by Francesco Redi and disproved spontaneous generation circa 1850. Redi's experiments were not accepted until Pasteur boiled some nutrient broth in a special glass with an S-curved neck. Nothing in the air was allowed to blow into the broth after it was sterilized, and therefore no new growth occurred. When one of these special flasks had the neck broken off, allowing air and dust to get into the chicken broth, mold then began growing on the surface. One of these flasks with the S-curved neck that Pasteur used in his experiment is still on display in a museum in France and shows no growth in over 150 years. Louis Pasteur rightly stated that "Life always comes from life." This is called the Law of Biogenesis. Note that this is called a law and not a theory.

Flat Earth? — Early Egyptians had proven the earth was round and had even calculated its circumference. Christopher Columbus believed that the earth was a sphere because of Isaiah 40:22: "God sits enthroned above the circle of the earth." From out in space, a sphere looks like a circle. The flat earth idea was made up by some local adversaries to discredit Columbus in his attempt to sail around the world to India.

Center of the Universe — The very best astronomers once believed that the earth was the center of the universe and that everything in space revolved around it. Copernicus, Kepler, Galileo, and Newton all helped to establish the correct cosmology. The brightest scientists of our time used to believe that man would never get to the moon or break the sound barrier. What scientists believe is truth is always changing unless it is based on God's Word. Jesus said, "I am the way, the TRUTH, and the life" (John 14:6, author's emphasis).

Scientific Predictions — The following are quotes from leading scientific experts in various fields of technology and their predictions for the future which were provided to me by Grady McMurtry. I have verified many of these at various websites, and although some may be urban legends, all of them will make you think.

"Louis Pasteur's theory of germs is ridiculous fiction." — Pierre Pachet, Professor of Physiology at Toulouse, 1872.

"The abdomen, the chest, and the brain will forever be shut from the intrusion of the wise and humane surgeon." — Sir John Eric Ericksen, British surgeon, appointed Surgeon-Extraordinary to Queen Victoria, 1873.

"Everything that can be invented has been invented." — Commissioner, U.S. Office of Patents, 1899.

"Drill for oil? You mean drill into the ground to try to find oil? You're crazy." — Drillers whom Edwin L. Drake tried to enlist to his project to drill for oil in 1859.

"Heavier-than-air machines are impossible." — Lord Kelvin, president of the Royal Society, 1895.

"Professor Goddard does not know the relation between action and reaction and the need to have something better than a vacuum against which to react. He seems to lack the basic knowledge ladled out daily in high schools." — 1921 *New York Times* editorial about Robert Goddard's revolutionary rocket work.

"Man will never reach the moon regardless of all future scientific advances." — Dr. Lee DeForest, inventor of the television.

"The bomb will never go off. I speak as an expert in explosives." — Admiral William Leahy, U.S. Atomic Bomb Project.

"There is no likelihood man can ever tap the power of the atom." — Robert Millikan, Nobel Prize in Physics, 1923.

"Stocks have reached what looks like a permanently high plateau" — Irving Fisher, Professor of Economics, Yale University, 1929.

"Computers in the future may weigh no more than 1.5 tons." — *Popular Mechanics*, forecasting the relentless march of science, 1949.

"Airplanes are interesting toys but of no military value." — Marechal Ferdinand Foch, Professor of Strategy, Ecole Superieure de Guerre.

"I think there is a world market for maybe five computers." — Thomas Watson, chairman of IBM, 1943.

"I have traveled the length and breadth of this country and talked with the best people, and I can assure you that data processing is a fad that won't last out the year." — The editor in charge of business books for Prentice Hall, 1957.

"But what . . . is it good for?" — Engineer at the Advanced Computing System Division of IBM, 1968, commenting on the microchip.

"There is no reason anyone would want a computer in their home." — Ken Olson, president, chairman, and founder of Digital Equipment Corp.,1977.

"640K ought to be enough for anybody." — Bill Gates.

"This 'telephone' had too many shortcomings to be seriously considered as a means of communication. The device is inherently of no value to us." — Western Union internal memo, 1876.

"The wireless music box has no imaginable commercial value. Who would pay for a message sent to nobody in particular?" — David Sarnoff's associates in response to his urgings for investment in the radio in the 1920s.

"If I had thought about it, I wouldn't have done the experiment. The literature was full of examples that said you can't do this." — Spencer Silver on the work that led to the unique adhesives for 3-M Post-It® Notepads.

These are excellent examples of how scientists' beliefs—their "truths"—are constantly changing.

XIV. Other Facts

Molecular Biology — Scientists have tried to use molecular biology to prove evolution. They wanted to find a correlation in protein relationships that would confirm their evolutionary hypothesis that "simple" life forms would have simple proteins and "complex" life forms would show increasing complexity. The comparison of protein relationships of various animals indicated that humans and lampreys (eel) are closer in these relationships than are fish and lampreys. This frustrated the scientists, since humans and lampreys are quite different species, and fish and lampreys are much closer species. This shows no increasing complexity of molecular biology with increasing complexity of life form. This is another enigma for the evolutionists.

Meteorites — Astronomers say that hundreds of meteorites hit the earth every year. If this has been true throughout the billions of years it supposedly took to lay down all the geologic column, we should see numerous meteorites in the sediments. But guess what? We don't see them. Why? Because the majority of the sediments were laid during the year of Noah's Flood.

Temple Of Amen-Ra — Around 2000 B.C., an Egyptian Pharaoh built the Solar Temple of Amen-Ra. On the longest day of the year, the summer solstice, the setting sun would reach far enough north to shine down the long corridor of the temple and illuminate the inner chamber, which was lined with gold. The Pharaoh would stand in the chamber as the sunlight entered and at that moment he would become one with the sun god. This practice is documented from historical records. The sun today, however, does not get far enough north to shine down the corridor. Furthermore, the measurements of the winter and summer solstice shadows taken by ancient astronomers were very precise except that the latitude was off by today's measurements. Much religious importance was attached to these measurements, and these ancient astronomers were probably very accurate in their recording of the latitude. Something has occurred to cause the shift in the latitude. Perhaps this could be explained by the wobble of the earth's axis.

Mount St. Helens — Psalm 104:32 says, "He looks at the earth, and it trembles; He touches the mountains and they smoke." These forces were seen on May 18, 1980, when Mount St. Helens in Washington state erupted. There the geological forces were observed to have worked at a very rapid rate. Fifty square miles of forest were wiped out in six minutes. Over 300 feet of material was deposited in Spirit Lake in about the same time. A wave of water over 800 feet high carved the rocks on the opposite side of the lake in seconds. Layers and formations called varves, that geologists say take millions of years to form, were formed in this one day. Subsequent to the eruption when a log jam on the Toutle River broke free, a canyon 100 feet deep and over 100 feet wide was eroded in one day through hard rock by the scouring of the mud flow (Ham 1993). It is called the Little Grand Canyon.

Lead 206 and Lead 207 — The "neutron capture" of lead theory proposed by Melvin Cook, a prize-winning geochemist, says that ^{206}Lead can capture free neutrons and form ^{207}Lead. This process was previously thought to work only in reverse. Cook's data suggests that most of the lead in the earth's crust could have formed this way, rather than from the decay series of ^{238}Uranium. Evolutionists use the ratio of ^{238}Uranium to ^{206}Lead and the half-life of ^{238}Uranium to indicate to them that the earth is very old. This neutron capture theory says that lead can go back and forth between its stable and unstable states. This would mean that any Uranium-to-Lead ratios would be meaningless in trying to determine the age of the earth.

Flow Rate of Basalt — The flow rate of basalt is very low (high viscosity), but it does flow, and the rate has been measured. The moon's material is very similar to earth's basalt, and if it were very old, those sharp crater rims on the moon would have flowed and flattened out over a long period of time. However, if the earth and the moon are very young, then the moon should retain the sharp crater rims that are observed. Again, the observable universe fits the Creation model.

Galaxy Clusters — Astronomers are perplexed by the clusters of galaxies in the universe. Nowhere are any single field galaxies seen. The galaxies should have dispersed in the supposed twenty billion years since the universe was formed if the universe were actually old and receding. If the universe is really only about 6,000 years old, then we would expect to see the galaxies still in clusters. "In the beginning, O Lord, you laid the foundations of the earth, and the heavens are the work of your hands" (Heb. 1:10). "The Son is the radiance of God's glory . . . sustaining all things by His powerful Word" (Heb. 1:3). God holds all things together.

Many arguments among astronomers have been bubbling since the Hubble telescope was repaired. Astronomers have continued to refine their measurements of the "Hubble constant" for determining distance and age. This revision means that it has never been a constant nor has it ever been agreed upon. New observations reveal very mature-looking galaxies in the very early universe. "This seeming inconsistency—objects that appear older than the inferred age of the universe—is commonly known as the age problem" (Peebles 1994). Because the universe holds together, astronomers believe that it must be full of cold dark matter. The following quote is an admission of truth: "Much of this extra material must consist of unseen dark matter of indeterminate nature, yet another uncomfortable unknown" (Peebles 1994).

Star Light — The speed of light today is 186,282 miles per second (or ~300,000,000 meters per second). When the sun, moon, and stars were created, their light very possibly reached the earth instantaneously. The lights in the sky were created "as signs and to mark the seasons and days and years . . . and to give light to the earth" (Gen. 1:14-15). There was no waiting around for years for the light from the nearest star (beyond our sun) to reach Earth. Using the speed of light to calculate the distance to far-away galaxies challenges the powers of science. The cosmological constant known as lambda is called, "the biggest problem in all of physics," according to an article in *Scientific American* (Peebles 1994).

Polystrate Fossils — Polystrate fossils are fossils that extend through many layers, and they pose a problem to evolutionary geologists. "The wisdom of this world is foolishness in God's sight" (1 Cor. 3:19). How could a tree trunk, for example, be incorporated in rocks that span millions of years of geologic time? The answer is that it couldn't. It was incorporated in a vast amount of sediment that was laid down in a single catastrophic event, the Flood. We can see evidence of this happening in Spirit Lake at Mount St. Helens (Ham, 1993).

CONCLUSION

"In the beginning was the Word, and the Word was with God, and the Word was God. He was with God in the beginning. Through him all things were made; without him nothing was made that has been made. In him was life, and that life was the light of men. The light shines in the darkness, but the darkness has not understood it" (John 1:1-5).

"Turn away from godless chatter and the opposing ideas of what is falsely called knowledge, which some have professed and in doing so have wandered from the faith" (1 Timothy 6:20-21).

There is a Creator and a Savior, and we need Him.

Jill Whitlock

Creation Science Outline
K-3

Outline:

I. Days of Creation
- A. Day One — Light and dark
- B. Day Two — Waters above and waters below
  1. Water vapor canopy
  2. Shielded harmful sun rays—longer life span (see timeline chart on page vi)
  3. Warm climate worldwide — no storms, no rain
  4. Fountains of the great deep
- C. Day Three — Dry land and plants
  1. Seas gathered in one place
  2. Land in one place with plants
- D. Day Four — Sun, moon, and stars
  1. Light before sun
  2. Stars for signs and to mark seasons, days, years
- E. Day Five — Fish and birds
- F. Day Six — All other animals and Man

II. Flood Geology and Noah's Ark
- A. Noah's Ark designed by God
- B. Water for the Flood came from the fountains of the great deep
- C. Mountains and other geological formations were formed during the Flood or soon after
  1. Tibetan Plateau
  2. Grand Canyon formed from a natural breached dam
  3. Volcanoes
- D. Earth's axis is tilted
  1. Now we have seasons
  2. Polar ice caps form
- E. Evidence for a worldwide Flood
  1. Fossils can only be preserved by rapid burial
  2. Fossils that go through many layers
  3. Earth is mostly covered with water

III. Young Earth Theory
- A. False age dating
- B. Not enough salt in the oceans
- C. Evidence from Grand Canyon and Mt. St. Helens

IV. Darwin's Theory Is False
- A. Fossils record supports separate classification of kinds
- B. No transitional creatures (plants or animals) are seen
- C. Mutations are harmful or neutral; very few are beneficial
- D. Animals always reproduce their own kind (i.e. dogs-dog; fish-fish; etc.)

V. Fossil Record
    A. Shows that animals stay the same or disappear
    B. No transition from jellyfish to fish or amphibian to reptile
    C. Fossil creatures look identical to the same creatures today

VI. Bad Science and Deliberate Hoaxes
    A. Neanderthal Man
    B. Piltdown Man — ape jaw was filed down and stained to look old
    C. Nebraska Man — man and family drawn from a single pig's tooth (!)
    D. Java Man — ape skull put with human leg bone, human skulls were hidden
    E. *Australopithecus* — probably extinct form of ape; name means "southern ape"

VII. What Scientists Believe Is Always Changing
    A. Earth is center of solar system
    B. Flies and rats come from garbage
    C. Maggots come from meat

VIII. Other Facts
    A. Mount St. Helens — showed rapid and massive erosion and deposition
    B. Galaxy clusters — Astronomers see only groups of galaxies. If the universe were very old, the galaxies should have scattered apart.

Lesson Plans

Subject	Monday	Tuesday	Wednesday	Thursday	Friday
Date:					
Bible/Religion Studies	Gen. 1:1-5	TS	Gen. 1:6-8	TS	TS
Creation Teaching Outline	I. A Creation Day One		I. B Day Two		
Reading Selection	Light and dark	TS	Waters above and waters below	TS	TS
Language Arts	Assign five words from list	Begin creating ABC book	Play card game with words	Begin nature diary	Tell about nature walk or write observations
Math Reinforcement		Calendar Skills Count days of Creation	Make applesauce muffins		Count legs of insects, etc.
Science Activities and Experiments Light & Dark Water	Big Bang Experiment	Experiments from light and dark	Make vapor canopy		Go on nature walk and observe God's creation
Geography/History World Map or Globe	Map Skills: identify continents		Hypothesize where the Garden of Eden might be located; find on map		Review continents; learn oceans
Art/Music		Use clip art or drawings for ABC book	Make musical instruments	Use various musical instruments	

CR= Creation Resource   TS= Teacher Selection

Lesson Plans

Week 2 — Days of Creation
K-3

Subject Date:	Monday	Tuesday	Wednesday	Thursday	Friday
Bible/Religion Studies	Gen. 1:9-13	TS	Gen. 1:14-19	TS	TS
Creation Teaching Outline	I. C. Day Three		I. D. Day Four		
Reading Selection	Dry land and plants	TS	Sun, moon, stars	TS	TS
Language Arts	Assign five words from list	Continue creating ABC book	Make vocabulary flash cards	Select vocabulary flash card game	Nature diary
Math Reinforcement	Fractions	Calendar; phases of moon	Bake or cook using fractions		Group items
Science Activities and Experiments Light & Dark Water	Grow plants from seeds	Rotation of the earth	Phases of the moon	Planets and order	Craters on moon
Geography/History World Map or Globe	Map Skills: identify continents and oceans	Northern and Southern hemispheres	Geographical terms using globe	Geographical terms using atlas	Review continents and oceans and other terms
Art/Music	Do salt painting	Use paper plates and beans percussion instrument	Use dry beans for picture of planets	Play scale on the recorder or other instrument	TS

CR= Creation Resource

TS= Teacher Selection

Lesson Plans

Subject Date:	Monday	Tuesday	Wednesday	Thursday	Friday
Bible/Religion Studies	Gen.1:20-23	Gen. 1:24-27	Gen. 1:27-31	Gen. 2:1-14	Gen. 2:15-25
Creation Teaching Outline	I. E. Day Five		I. F. Day Six		God rested
Reading Selection	Fish and birds	TS	All other animals and man	TS	TS
Language Arts	Assign five words from list	Continue creating ABC book	Play a vocabulary card game	Write or retell Creation story	Write nature poem
Math Reinforcement	Categorize types of animals		Measure body proportions	What shape are you?	TS
Science Activities and Experiments Birds and Fish Animals and Man	Food chain	Learn about flight	Blindfold activity	Camouflage	Bone and calcium activity
Geography/History World Map or Globe	Map skills: chart bird migration	Draw a map of yard or a room to scale	Research early civilizations and locate on map	Compass activity	Navigate outdoors activity
Art/Music	Make different animal sounds and record	Days of Creation mobile	Record scales or other musical instrument into recorder	String letter beads into a necklace	TS

CR= Creation Resource

TS= Teacher Selection

Lesson Plans

Week 4 —The Flood and Noah's Ark
K-3

Subject / Date:	Monday	Tuesday	Wednesday	Thursday	Friday
Bible/Religion Studies	Gen. 3:1-24	Gen. 6: 5-8	Gen. 7: 1-23	Gen. 8: 1-22 Gen. 9-1-29	Job 40:15-18 Ps. 104:26, Is. 27:1
Creation Teaching Outline	II.	II. A.	II. B.	II. C.	II. D.
Reading Selection	Flood geology	Noah's Ark	Water from flood	Mountains	Earth's axis and evidence of Flood
Language Arts	Assign five words from list	Continue creating ABC book	Write or dictate animal story and Ark	Retell story of Ark and Flood	Play "What am I?" game
Math Reinforcement	Count animals on ark 2 x 2	Learn to count by 2's, 3's, etc.	Divide animals into groups	Use tokens or animals for math problems	TS
Science Activities and Experiments Flood/Floating/Sinking Dinosaurs	Make boat, fill with animals: float or sink?	Demo rain activity	Water cycle illustrate and explain	Study oceans	Dino Activity: chicken bone and plaster
Geography/History World Map or Globe	Map skills: identify Mt. Ararat and Mesopotamia region		Look at shapes of continents: would they fit together?		Study topographical map
Art/Music	Make clay or cookie dough animals	Sounds of flood music	Create stormy flood scene picture	Fill glasses with water and play scale	TS

CR= Creation Resource

TS= Teacher Selection

Lesson Plans

Subject Date:	Monday	Tuesday	Wednesday	Thursday	Friday
Bible/Religion Studies	Gen. 11: 1-9		Gen. 11:10-26		Gen. 12:1-3
Creation Teaching Outline	III.	IV.	V.	VI.	
Reading Selection	Young earth theory	Darwin's false theory	Fossil record	Bad science	
Language Arts	Assign five words from list	Continue creating ABC book	Bunny hop game	Observe details of Creation; write or draw	Open-ended story
Math Reinforcement	Fractions; baking or cooking	Slice fruit; study more fractions	Shapes and geometry	Orderliness of creation: find examples	Math shortcuts
Science Activities and Experiments	Rotation of the earth	Weather	Worldwide Flood; make rain	Water cycle	TS
Geography/History World Map or Globe	Formations; Grand Canyon	Continents, Oceans	Other nations' flood accounts	Erosion of Niagara Falls	Erosion of sea sediment
Art/Music	Study the orchestra	Vegetable prints	Study the instruments in the orchestra	String letter beads	TS

CR= Creation Resource

TS= Teacher Selection

Lesson Plans

Subject / Date:	Monday	Tuesday	Wednesday	Thursday	Friday
Bible/Religion Studies	TS————————————————————————————————→				
Creation Teaching Outline	VII.		VIII.		
Reading Selection	What scientists believe is changing		Other facts		
Language Arts	Review and add remaining words	Complete creating ABC book	Complete nature book	LA assignment	Play vocabulary bop or bingo
Math Reinforcement	Draw star of David	Count insect or other creature legs	Math solutions game	Draw circles and observe	TS
Science Activities and Experiments	Stalactites & stalagmites	Big Bang	Entropy; disorder	Adaptation and variation within species	
Geography/History Ideas World Map or Globe	Map skills: review geographical terms and places	Research scientists	Complete any activities from previous weeks		
Art/Music	Listen to classical music	Make snack necklace	Identify instruments from various types of music	Pipe cleaner or sand art	Paper folding art

CR= Creation Resource   TS= Teacher Selection

Reading List
K-3

Some Christian books, marked with asterisks, may be difficult to find in the library. Use the list of additional resources on page 140 to find these highly recommended titles.

Read Aloud

Bomby: The Bombardier Beetle by H. M. Rue and Richard Bliss (Master Books, 1984, 40 pages). This is an amazing beetle that fires cannon blasts at its foes. Playful, informative and fun. Remarkable evidence for design.

* *The Creation When God Made the World* edited by John D. Morris (Master Books, 1998, 36 pages). Use this beautifully illustrated book to discuss how the universe, planets, and living beings came into existence. Highly recommended for your library.

Dinosaur ABC's Activity Book by Richard Bliss (Master Books, 1986, 29 pages). A children's coloring and activity book loaded with information about how dinosaurs fit into the Bible.

Fossils, Frogs, Fish and Friends by K. Ernst and Richard Bliss (Master Books,1984, 28 pages). Two friends discuss their fascination with the fossil record and the Great Flood.

Fossils: Hard Facts From the Earth by Norman Fox and Richard Bliss (Master Books, 1981, 32 pages). A well-documented and realistic approach to the fossil record.

Life Before Birth by Gary Parker (Creation Life Publications, 1993, 85 pages). A Biblical look at the birth process and reproduction. Use your own discretion regarding when to introduce your children to this topic.

The Magic School Bus Inside the Earth by Joanna Cole (Scholastic, Inc., 1987, 40 pages). This book will help the children understand and remember the scientific vocabulary because of the silly way the information is presented.

Independent Reading

A is For Adam by Ken and Mally Ham (Master Books, 1995, 118 pages). This book presents the ABCs and the Gospel in rhymes. The back section of the book has black line reproducible pages of each of the colored pages at the beginning of the book that kids will love to color!

D is for Dinosaur by Ken and Mally Ham (Master Books, 1991, 123 pages). The book is divided into halves. The first half is rhyming letters of the alphabet and includes funny dinosaur pictures. The second half contains drawings ready for coloring, plus notes on dinosaurs and exercises for each rhyme.

Dry Bones and Other Fossils by Gary Parker (Master Books, 1995, 72 pages). Four children look to a knowledgeable parent in this book that will delight children with the world of fossils and the Flood that caused them.

The "God Created" Series by Earl & Bonnie Snellenberger (Master Books, 1989, 32 pages). An assortment of coloring books with stickers and reproducible black-line pages.

Hummy and the Wax Castle by Elizabeth Ernst and Richard B. Bliss (Master Books, 1984, 54 pages). The amazing evidence of design found among the bees, written as a narrative for children. Contains striking illustrations.

Noah's Ark by Peter Spier (Doubleday, 1977, 32 pages). Children will love this picture book of a well-known story.

What Really Happened to the Dinosaurs by John Morris and Ken Ham (Master Books, 1990, 32 pages). Highly imaginative book takes young readers on a pre-Flood journey through God's creation. A fun-filled adventure with Tracker John and his pet dinosaur.

Resources

Genesis for Kids: Science Experiments That Show God's Power in Creation! by Doug Lambier and Robert Stevenson (Tommy Nelson, 1997, 160 pages). Experiments dealing with light, air, and water; land, plants, and the sea; the sun; moon; the birds and the fish; animals; and people.

How Nature Works by David Burnie (Dorling Kindersley, 1991, 192 pages). While several activities deal with evolution (our teaching outline will combat any questions you may have!), this book nevertheless has very good experiments dealing with nature.

How the Earth Works by John Farndon (Dorling Kindersley, 1991, 192 pages). For a great book with earth science experiments, this one fits the bill. Beautiful color photos throughout and easy-to-perform experiments.

Streams of Civilization, Volume One by Albert Hyma and Mary Stanton (Creation-Life Publishers, 1992, 410 pages). A very good and comprehensive romp through history from the dawn of the world to A.D.1294! This book is written from a Creationist perspective and was actually sponsored by the Institute for Creation Research. A must-have.

Maps and Globes by Jack Knowlton (Thomas Y. Crowell, 1985, 42 pages). A great book for the younger crowd. (Any good atlas or globe will do.)

Vocabulary/Spelling List

K-3

	rain		flood
	Noah		Genesis
	creation		sun
	moon		stars
	light		dark
	water		animals
	dinosaurs		ark
	Old Testament		kinds
	reproduce		mutation
	lies		deliberate
	meteor		volcano
	galaxy		vapor
	earth		canopy
	preserve		bubble
	shielding		rays
	climate		storms
	plants		sea
	land		continent
	geology		fossil
	poles		ice cap
	old		young
	shrinking		receding

Vocabulary/Spelling/Grammar Ideas
K-3

† Use the vocabulary words as spelling words for older children. You may assign five or more words per week. Add to this list as the need arises and you find words that you would like your children to learn to spell or define. For younger children, concentrate on having them become familiar with the vocabulary words. Here are some activities and games to incorporate the vocabulary/spelling words into your unit study.

† Have children use the words in sentences to show they know the spelling and meaning. Younger children can use the words in sentences or stories. Have them read the sentences into a tape recorder or dictate them to an adult or older child, who can then write them on large tablets of paper. Have the children "read" back their sentences.

† Have young children (K) pick out the alphabet letters they are studying. Rewrite the vocabulary words in large bold print on an erasable surface or on paper. Have them circle the letters they are learning (all the A's, B's, and C's, etc.).

† Choose one or two of the children's "best" sentences and have them recopy them using their neatest handwriting. (Give them a model to copy if they are just learning to print or write.)

† Use the sentences the children have written to label the parts of speech. Use colored pencils or markers for this activity. Color and code each part of speech as follows:

  Underline the nouns once in red.
  Underline the verbs twice in blue.
  Draw a squiggly line under the adjectives.
  Draw a purple box around the prepositions.
  (Continue this pattern with other parts of speech you are studying.)

† Make vocabulary flash cards. A parent or student may create these cards. One side contains the word and the other the definition. Use these cards to practice. Once the vocabulary has been learned, you may play various games with the cards. You can play against your child. If he successfully defines a word, he keeps the card; if he doesn't, you get the card. Play go fish: place a paper clip on each card, then spread them on the floor. Using a strong magnet, fish for the cards. If the definition is facing upward the word must be recited, or vice-versa.

† Use the vocabulary words for younger children to make picture books. The children can cut pictures out of magazines or draw pictures to illustrate the words. Place the words in alphabetical order.

† Have the children take the largest words and find small words within them. Have them list the words in alphabetical order.

† Play "Vocabulary Bop." Inflate various size balloons. Write the vocabulary words on the balloons with black marker. Have each child keep a balloon up in the air and tell what the word means before it touches the ground. They may keep the ones (balloons) they answer correctly. The child with the most balloons wins. If you don't want to inflate many balloons you can add the correct words to the balloon and add the total words at the end of the game appearing on each balloon. Variation: "Spelling Bop." Have the children hit the balloon up in the air while they are spelling the word. If the word is correct they may keep the balloon.

† Use a saltbox to practice writing. Place a sheet of black construction paper into a shallow box, then cover with salt. Trace letters in the salt with your finger.

† Make an ABC book with the words from this study guide. Use one page for each letter and cut out pictures from magazines, draw pictures, use clip art or find art from other sources.

† String letter beads to make words relating to this study. Be creative or use the words on the vocabulary list.

† Have your child face a marker board or chalk board. Using the vocabulary list trace the letters on the child's back for each word and let him write the letters on the board. Once you are finished, check to see if the words are correct.

† Using letter tiles try to spell out some of the vocabulary words you might have difficulty spelling. Select letter tiles to spell several of the vocabulary words and ten blank tiles. Turn the tiles upside down and play spelling solitaire. Turn over the tiles one by one until you make your words.

† Make a photocopy of the vocabulary list and examine the words. Have younger children circle specific letters. Older students may circle the vowels. Try to determine the part of speech for each word.

† Using one of the language arts writing activities in the next section, search for grammatical errors. Is the punctuation correct? It sometimes helps to put away the lesson for a day or two and then read it.

† Have students cut pictures out of an old magazine or sales flyers (I keep a stack of these) to illustrate their spelling words. Put them in a 3-ring binder with specific pages for the letters of the alphabet. Before long they will have their own illustrated dictionary.

† This activity is better done outdoors. Have the children form a line, standing shoulder to shoulder. Using the vocabulary words, question the children, giving them only the definitions; for example, "This is the name of the planet on which we live." If they get the

word correct, they may take a baby step, giant step, two bunny hops, etc. The first person to reach the designated finish line is the winner. The size of the steps is dependent on the ease or difficulty of the word. You may have the "step" designations on slips of paper, and the child must draw a slip before moving (or the parent may do this for the child).

 Using the vocabulary words, play a game with analogies or opposites. For example, the opposite of land is sea, the opposite of young is old.

Language Arts
K-3

✝ These suggestions may help you incorporate language arts into your unit study. Remember to use these ideas as a jumping-off point. Many times the specific suggestions may not appeal to you but will instead give you a better idea! Often parents e-mail me with comments or suggestions—some of which are incorporated into this book.

✝ With young children language arts should include verbal expression such as telling back a story using their own words (narration). Children also love to tell stories about events, places, things or people they've met. If they cannot write, have them tell the story to you. Simply write down or type the stories, correcting only enough to make the sentences readable. They may illustrate the story using clip art or their own drawings. With a little practice, many children will take pleasure from this activity.

✝ When God created during the Creation week, He said certain aspects were good. We can see the goodness of God's Creation even today. To appreciate it, go on a nature hike and really notice the detail of little things. Use a magnifying glass for this activity. Look at flower petals, blades of grass, the bark of a tree, etc. Describe what you see, and keep a nature journal. Do this same activity several times during one week. Do you notice any changes?

✝ Write a poem about Creation. Try to keep the poem to seven lines, each one dealing with one of the days of Creation. You may use a specific poetry technique.

✝ Read Genesis 1:14-19 to the children, then make up a fun rhyme or poem such as the following using hand motions to illustrate the story: The sun shines in the sky all day....It never asks anything of us....Even if we can't visit the sun...The sun shines its light on us.

✝ Discuss the word "creation" and explain that it means to make something (in God's case to make something from nothing!). Explain that painting a picture or making up a story is creating. Then proceed to "create."

✝ God created light, and there are also man-made versions of light. List these on a sheet of paper; see how many you can come up with. Variation: Give the children an old magazine or catalog and have them cut out pictures of things that give light.

✝ On the fourth day God made the sun. Write a haiku (a type of poetry) about the sun. Give the first line five syllables, second line seven syllables, and third line five syllables.

✝ Read your favorite book about Noah's Ark or read Genesis 6-8 in a children's Bible. Have your children pretend they are on Noah's Ark. What would they say or do? How would they feel in an ark with all those animals? Have them draw a picture of themselves in the Ark and write down their comments. Read the book again including their comments.

† Tape record (or videotape) the above activity with the additional dialogue. Have them make animal sounds for the background noises!

† Choose a paragraph from a children's Bible. Write this paragraph neatly and have the children copy it. Dictate the paragraph to older children once they are familiar with it. Have them check their work. This may take some practice! Variation: read the passage and have the children retell the event in their own words.

† Have the children choose different types of animals and describe them orally using as many creative descriptions as possible. You may want to list some of these on a marker board or paper. Once this is completed, you may want to take turns describing a specific animal without saying its name while others try to guess the kind of animal. Another spin-off game is "What am I?" Here the child lists a maximum of three characteristics of the animal such as, "I live in a jungle, I eat meat, and have a scary roar. What am I?"

† Have the children pretend they are animals on Noah's Ark. Have them describe the following: How do they feel when they leave the Ark? What does the post-Flood world look like? What types of food do they eat? Where do they go to live?

† Begin an open-ended story and take turns adding to the story orally. (This is especially fun with a group of different-aged children.) For example: "One day while I was riding my black pony I heard a loud cry. There in the distance I saw a boy chasing a dinosaur. I couldn't believe my eyes! I galloped quickly in his direction when suddenly…." You may want to tape record some of these sessions. The children will really enjoy listening to this later.

† If your children could ask any of the following people questions what would they be? List the questions and play-act or write the scene. Choose from these people or select your own: God the Father, Adam, Eve, Moses, etc.

† Have your children explain how they would have felt if they had been the first person created with only a beautiful land and animals and no other people. What would they like to happen next?

† Create a scrapbook with items collected during a unit study. Have the children write about specific activities, illustrating them or using memorabilia from nature walks, field trips, or even online resources. Have them print out online graphics with your help. Type in "free graphics" on a family-safe search engine (or one with safety controls).

† Play an alphabet game focusing on the Creation account; for example, "My name is Adam and I am going to Alabama and I am taking some apples…." Do this with each letter of the alphabet and bring in as much of the Genesis account as possible.

† True or false? Some of the concepts about evolution taught in science books on the library shelf are not provable. Have the children identify the difference between true and false phrases. You can really have fun with this activity. Use the teaching outline to give you some ideas. Have them dictate or write sentences, and you write some, too. Then take the test. For example: Bumblebees live in cars. T/F? Cats have fur. T/F? God created the world in six days and rested on the seventh. T/F? Shem is the name of one the men that built the ark. T/F?

Math Reinforcements
K-3

† Count the days of Creation. How many hours are in each day? Does this include night? How many minutes are in one hour? How many seconds? Make a clock. Using poster board, cut hands for the clock out of bright colors. Use different colors for minute and second hands and fasten with a clasp in the center. Learn how to tell time.

† "Count" Noah's animals. Draw animals or use toy ones. Learn to count by 2's, 3's, 4's, etc. Count from 0 to 100 by 2's.

† Divide the animals into groups of two, three, four, etc. Show the relation of multiplication to sets. Have them count different sets. Is it easier to add or multiply? Try adding ten 2's together. Now try multiplying 10 x 2. Which is easier?

† Use the animals or tokens (make your own or use toy cars, blocks, etc.) for addition and subtraction.

† Go on a nature walk and look for insects that have legs. Count their legs, and keep a chart of the insects according to the number of legs they have. Try to find spiders, grasshoppers, and a centipede!

† Study an ant hill. (Be careful—ants bite!) Count the number of ants you can see in five minutes. How many ants do you think are in the ant hill? Estimate.

† Talk about the trees in the Garden of Eden. Take an apple and demonstrate fractions. Cut it in half, fourths, eighths, etc. Use this concept with other fruit. Eat the fruit!

† Make applesauce muffins or another recipe using apples. Note the different measurements used. Have children compare the fractions of solids with liquid fractions. Baking is a great way to teach children about measurements and fractions.

† Make applesauce muffins without any measuring devices. Teach fractions and the importance of accurate measuring.

† Thinking of easy solutions to discover the answers to math problems can be fun. Look for math shortcuts. For example, one plus any number is the next number in the series. Two plus any number, is two more. Any number between 1 and 9 added to 9 is that number less 1, and 1 added in the tens column before it. For example 9 + 8= ?. Take the 8, subtract 1 (that would be 7) and add a 1 in the tens column. The answer is 17. The problem 8 + 7 would be 7 less 2 is 5, with a 1 in the tens column, or 15. This takes a bit of practice, but children quickly catch on. Doubles can be easy to remember for little children after a bit of practice. That leaves very few of the middle addition facts, the 3's— 4's— 5's—6's to memorize!

† Make a chart of addition facts and color in the facts as your children learn them. Making a big poster is fun so the children have a visual and goal to work toward.

† Noah had to do a lot of measuring to build the Ark. Use a ruler first, then a tape measure to become familiar with measuring items. Give your child a list of various items to measure and chart the results. Even a reluctant math student will enjoy this activity.

† The following suggested activities are adapted from *Math Wizardry for Kids* by Margaret Kenda and Phyllis S. Williams (Barrons, 1995). We highly recommend this book.

† God is a God of order. Mathematics illustrates this. Draw various sizes of circles. As long as they are all circles they have something very important in common. They are all round! The only way they can be different is in size. (See math, grades 4-8 on page 88 for additional circle mathematical activities proving this phenomenon.)

† Shapes have mathematical properties. When Noah built the Ark, it was designed to withstand the ravages of the flood. God obviously understood geometric principles! Try drawing mathematical shapes. First draw a triangle. Now shade the "mirror image" of the triangle. Once you have done this, if it is the exact size of the triangle you drew, you will notice that it makes a four-sided shape known as a parallelogram. Note: The parallelogram will be standing on end.

† More geometry: If you draw a triangle and an inverse triangle over it you have a star. It is known as the star of David and is the Jewish symbol. Try drawing other stars. How many points do they contain?

† Mathematics continues to prove the orderliness of God's Creation. An ancient Greek sculptor named Phidias believed that the perfect human body was 7½ heads tall. Measure the length of your head and then the length of your body. What is your proportion? Measure an adult. See if you can find someone that fits within Phidias's perfect or "golden proportion," as it was known by the Greeks.

† Find out what shape fits you. Stand as tall as you can and have someone measure your height from head to toe. Record this number. Next, stand with your arms outstretched. Measure the distance from the fingertips on one hand to the fingertips on the other. Record this number. Which category do you fall into? A rectangle or square? Make a chart with the following headings—adults, kids, babies—and record which each falls into.

Science Activities and Experiments
K-3

Science activities and experiments are lots of fun! Usually, it is best to tie in experiments with a specific topic. In this case, however, Creation encompasses everything, so it will be difficult to concentrate on experiments that tie in with one specific concept. It will therefore be important to continually discuss what you are learning! You can plan your science experiments using the six days of Creation and doing a science activity or experiment that fits in with what God created on each day. (See the Teaching Outline.) Using the scientific method makes the concept easier to understand. The **scientific method** is asking a question and finding the solution. Once you ask the question, make sure the children give you their hypothesis (or "guess" for younger children). This is what they think will happen. If they have no idea, read or observe to further research the question. The older children can write their experiment using the science experiment sheets found in the copy section of this book. The younger children can draw their answers. **Always use caution when doing any science activities or experiments! Parental supervision is a must!**

You may wish to set up experiments under the headings of the Creation week. To do, this plan activities and experiments for Light and Dark; Waters Above and Waters Below; Dry Land and Plants; Sun, Moon, and Stars; Birds and Fish; Animals and Man.

Light and Dark

† Demonstrate the three states of matter: solid, liquid, and gas. Use water: freeze it (solid), pour it (liquid), and boil it until there is steam (gas). Have the children write up an experiment sheet before doing each one of these activities.

† Blindfold activity: We take our eyes for granted. In a living room area place an object (such as a small ball) on a low table or on the floor. Go to the farthest end of the room. Take turns blindfolding each other and trying to navigate the room without using your eyes to obtain the ball. Variation of this activity: use oral directions to guide the blindfolded person.

† What color is light? Use a prism. If one is not available, on a nice sunny day take a garden hose outdoors and spray the water, allowing the sunlight to filter through the mist. What do you see? Record your observations. Why does this happen? Remember this name: Roy G. Biv, which stands for red, orange, yellow, green, blue, indigo, and violet (the colors of a rainbow).

† Light wave demonstration: Use a television remote control and a small, hand-held mirror. With your back to a television set (which is turned off), aim the remote into the mirror and try to turn on the TV set. Try this from different points in the room. Why does this happen? (The infrared rays in the remote send a signal to the sensor in your TV set. The mirror reflects this ray.)

† What is air? You can demonstrate the strength of air by using a balloon, a table, and a stack of books. Tie two or three books together with yarn or string. Place the stack of books on

top of a deflated balloon, letting the neck of the balloon hang over the table. Blow up the balloon. What happens to the books?

† Carbon dioxide is what is contained in both fire extinguishers and the fizz in soft drinks. You can demonstrate its firefighting properties with this experiment. Place a tablespoon of baking soda into a small-necked bottle and add three tablespoons of white vinegar. A chemical reaction will form between the soda and vinegar, creating carbon dioxide. Use this gas (tip the bottle to release the gas) and try to extinguish a lighted candle. Does it work?

† Demonstrate how important light is for plant growth. Place one plant in a sunny spot and place another in a dark place. Compare the results after three days and again after seven days. You may water the plants as needed. What does this tell us about the importance of the light God created?

† The Big Bang Experiment. Use a paper bag and some popsicle sticks. Place the sticks at the bottom of the bag and blow the bag up. Pop the bag as forcefully as you can and shake the sticks over the ground. What happens? Do the sticks create anything? Why not? (Order cannot be created out of disorder.)

Waters Above and Waters Below
† Demonstrate the vapor canopy by constructing a model. Use different types of recyclable materials. For example, you could surround a volleyball with plastic wrap.

† Demonstrate a vapor canopy. Use a solution of 8 tablespoons of liquid dish soap in 1 quart of water. Make a ring out of a 3-5-foot length of heavy twine and put it through a 1-2-foot length of PVC pipe or other tubing for a handle. Let the twine and handle soak in the soapy solution for 20-30 seconds, then pull the twine up into the air, moving it rapidly to make a very large bubble. When you get good at it, try putting a globe inside a bubble.

Dry Land and Plants
† What is a flood? Do you know of any areas that have flooded? What happens when there is a flood? How did this affect the people at the time of Noah?

† Study weather. Make a chart of the weather conditions with these headings: date, rainy, cloudy, sunny, windy, temperature. Keep track of the weather on a daily basis for a month or two.

† Study the rotation of the earth. What is an axis? What does this have to do with day and night? Study the orbit of the earth around the sun. What does this have to do with the months, years, and seasons? Make up your own calendar.

† Study the relationship of the moon to the earth. How does that relationship affect the tides?

Get a calendar with the tides plotted on it. You can find one in a store that sells fishing equipment.

† Make a boat out of an old margarine tub or other plastic container (Styrofoam food tray, etc.). Allow the "boat" to float in some water. Begin filling it with small toy animals. How many animals does it take to make the boat sink? Read Genesis 6:14-21. How did God's design for the Ark keep it from sinking with all the animals on board?

† Study the oceans. What types of animals are found in the oceans? Make a chart grouping them according to "kinds" (whales, dolphins, fish, seals, jellyfish, shellfish, seahorses, etc.).

† Draw a water cycle. Follow a drop of rain as it goes through the cycle. (See *Ranger Rick's NatureScope Wild About Weather.*)

† Demonstrate rain. Take a large jar with a lid (a mayonnaise jar works well) and a few ice cubes. Pour 1/2 cup water into the jar to cover the bottom. Put the lid upside down over the mouth of the jar and fill it with the ice cubes. Observe the underside of the lid. What happens? (See *Earth Science for Every Kid.*)

† Some of the craters on the Earth as well as the moon can be attributed to meteorites. These objects enter our atmosphere with a tremendous amount of speed, pulled by gravity. Do a demonstration to explain this event. Line a shallow tray with white flour and sprinkle paprika over the entire surface. Using small rocks, pebbles, or marbles, drop these "meteors" onto the surface and carefully lift them out (without causing more of an indentation than the object if possible). Observe the surface. What do you see?

† "Create" your own world…make a terrarium. Use a glass aquarium (ten gallons or larger), gravel, charcoal, potting soil, and humidity-loving plants such as ferns, mosses, and small flowering species of plants. If necessary, ask your local gardening center to help you with the items you will require. If you live in an area where you can find these things in nature use this method to collect the suggested items and add some of your own. Layer one-half inch of gravel, sprinkle a layer of charcoal, and add two inches of damp potting soil over this. Use a few plants, ferns, rocks, or small stones to complete your world. Spray the plants with a mister, and cover the top of the aquarium with foil. Set the aquarium in indirect light away from a heater. It will thrive with a minimum amount of care.

† Grow plants from seeds. Plant a bean seed (or other fast-growing plant) in a small glass jar. Line with a paper towel and place sand in the middle. Place the seed between the paper towel and the glass. Water the seeds by placing the water in the sand. Do this daily but do not over water. Make sure the soil is moist, not wet to the touch. Watch the plant grow. Variation: grow sprouts such as bean or broccoli sprouts. Not only are they fast-growing, but they are also nutritious!

Sun, Moon and Stars

ϯ   The Sun is the perfect distance away from the Earth to warm our planet. Make a model of the sun and all the planets that rotate around it: Mercury, Venus, Earth, Mars, Jupiter, Saturn, Uranus, Neptune, and Pluto.

ϯ   Examine a calendar that lists the phases of the moon. Watch the moon each night and chart its phase on the calendar. Is the calendar correct?

ϯ   Lie outside in the evening when it is really dark and look at the stars in the sky. On the first night, just look at all the stars. The next night use a resource to help you find and identify some of the constellations. Try not to use a light source, as it takes thirty minutes or more for your eyes to get acclimated to the dark. Cover a flashlight with red cellophane if you must use one. This will not affect your eyesight.

ϯ   Cook with the power of the sun. Use aluminum foil, a shoe box, and marshmallows to "cook" by solar power. Line a shoe box with foil and place several marshmallows on tooth picks in the bottom of the box. If necessary puncture small holes in the box so the toothpicks will stand upright. Place this box in the hot sun and watch what happens. Come back to the box every few minutes to check the progress. Eat the marshmallows between graham crackers and chocolate squares for a yummy treat.

ϯ   Have your children watch the moon while traveling in a car. What does the moon appear to be doing? (Following the car.) Why does this appear to be happening? Explain that the moon is a great distance away from the car.

ϯ   Gravity keeps us firmly on the earth's surface. Demonstrate the pull of gravity by dropping various objects from a second-story window or balcony. Use foil and paper for this demonstration. Crumble a piece of used computer paper and keep one piece flat. Drop both at the same time. What happens? Now try this same activity with a sheet of foil (use the same size for these experiments). Compare a sheet of foil to a piece of paper. Now compare a crumbled sheet of foil to a crumpled sheet of paper. Explain what happens.

ϯ   Centrifugal force is a real phenomenon, and this demonstration will make it more understandable to children. Use a bucket of water (a small beach pail will do). Tie a length of string to the handle of the pail and take turns swinging this around in a wide circle. Now, fill the pail half full of water and swing it around again. What happens? If you do this activity and slow down, what happens? You can compare this to the Earth's rotation which is "just right"; if it were too slow or too fast the Earth would not be inhabitable for man. God's Creation is perfect!

ϯ   Make a balloon rocket. Use string, tape, straws and balloons for this activity. Tape a straw to a deflated balloon, making sure that you leave enough room for expansion of the balloon. Place the string through the straw and tie each end to a tree (or have two children hold each end taut). Blow up the balloon and let go. Watch the "rocket" take off! You may try this activity by inflating the balloon and using a clothespin to secure the end. Thread the string through the straw and take the clothespin off when you are ready to launch your rocket. Be creative and try your own methods.

† Punch holes in the bottom of a paper cup to resemble the Little Dipper. Go into a dark room and shine a flashlight through the bottom of the cup onto a wall. What do you see? Do this with other constellations and make your own planetarium.

Birds and Fish

† Study a group of animals (fish, birds, insects, etc.). Learn about their habitats and eating habits.

† Photograph or draw as many different kinds of animals as you can, or cut out pictures from magazines.

† What is a food chain? Make a small drawing or a large poster depicting this chain.

† Take a walk on the beach and study the birds. Watch seagulls, pelicans, and sandpipers at work. What do they have in common? Animals have common attributes because they all have the same Creator!

† Learn about flight. How was man given the idea to fly? Watch the gracefulness of birds and research the way in which different birds flap their wings.

† Go on a nature walk and look for a variety of birds. How many did you find? List them using a good field guide for identification. Binoculars would be a help but are not necessary.

† There is such a wide variety of bird species. One particular bird, the anhinga, dives into the water to capture a fish, then rests on a nearby tree branch with its large black wings outspread to dry before it can fly again. How is this dangerous for the bird? Study some other birds and their odd behavior.

† Some things float and some things sink. Demonstrate this. Put items with about the same weight but different shapes (for example a toy boat and a ball) into a sink full of water. Try different items and watch the results. Two items that weigh the same may behave differently: one may sink and the other float. The item with the larger bottom surface, such as a boat, will normally float. Keep a record of what floats and what sinks.

Animals and Man

† Many animals are masters of camouflage. Take turns hiding a toy animal in the living area of your home in a spot that will camouflage it and having another person find the creature. You may use clues such as hot or cold to help the person find the item. Study how animals use camouflage as a way to survive.

† Calcium in our bones helps to strengthen them. As we age we lose calcium; and sometimes adults take calcium supplements. See what will happen when a bone loses calcium. Wash a chicken bone from dinner to remove all of the meat, then place it in a clean jar with a lid and add one cup of white vinegar (or enough to cover the bone). Place the lid on the jar and leave it in a cool place. Allow it to stand for five days. Take the bone out and examine it. What happened? Does the bone bend without breaking? If not, leave it in the jar for a longer period of time.

† Go outdoors and close your eyes. (You may use a blindfold if you desire.) Listen quietly to the sounds around you for five minutes. Document all the sounds you hear. List them in two specific categories: man-made (cars, planes, a door shutting) and those made by nature (birds, wind, leaves rustling). Which category contained the most?

† We are created with internal senses that warn us of danger. Demonstrate this by using various sounds. Give three or more children one device each to make a sound, such as a bell, a can with a stick, or an aluminum pie pan and a spoon. Make sure the sounds are different enough. Choose one sound that a blindfolded child must walk toward. Each child plays his sound, and the blindfolded child must listen and walk toward the correct sound.

† Many times creatures that appear to be a nuisance are really beneficial to mankind. Explain some beneficial animals. What would happen if some of these animals became extinct?

† God created everything for a purpose. Look at symbiotic relationships. Explain how these work. Describe the symbiotic relationship within a family.

† We learn about animals of the past from the fossil record. This is found in rocks that once were soft but became hard over time and with the right conditions. Demonstrate a fossil dig using plaster of Paris and a chicken bone. Mix the plaster according to the box directions and place several pieces of chicken bone in the wet plaster. When it hardens, turn out the mold and use this as a "paleontological" site. To excavate your site use popsicle sticks, a toothbrush, and an eyedropper with vinegar to speed up the process (the acidity in the vinegar will eat away at the plaster). Older children may use sharper devices, but be careful! You may draw grids if this is for upper elementary. The students should have a piece of paper with grids and then chart on their paper where they found a specific section of bone.

† Research early scientists whose belief in the Holy Scriptures aided them in the search for scientific truth. Research Johannes Kepler, Francis Bacon, Blaise Pascal, etc.

† Good nutrition is vital for our health. Food gives us the energy our bodies need to function well. God made our food good and pure, yet modern research has sometimes altered fruits and vegetables (GMO, genetically modified organisms). Instead of being beneficial, some are actually harmful, or worse, the results to humankind are as yet unknown. Research organic foods. What is the difference between food that is grown and certified as organic and food that is not? Compare, for example, organic milk with regular milk. You can find organic products in most grocery stores. A good website for information about organic foods and many other things is www.mercola.com.

† Experiment with healthy eating. Substitute sweet fruits such as apples or peaches for sweet treats for one day, and see if eating fruit will curb your desire for a cookie. See if you can do this for two, three, or four days or a week. Try to eliminate as many processed foods as possible. (You know a food is processed if it has a large string of additives or preservatives on the ingredients label.) Eat as many fresh fruits and vegetables as possible. Eating healthy doesn't mean you can never have a cookie or piece of cake, but it does mean that processed foods should not be the focus of your meals!

† To carry on maintenance and repairing processes, our bodies need a balance of nutrients such as proteins, carbohydrates, fats, minerals, and vitamins. Chart your meals for one week using the previous list as category headings. List the food items under each category and see if you are eating a balanced diet. If you are not, attempt to change this. Study good nutrition and diet.

More Fun Experiments and Activities

† Demonstrate sedimentary erosion. Place items in a large box or baking pan or do outdoors in a sandbox or at the beach. Use sand, rocks, pine needles, or other items found in nature and create a dam. Try to build up one area and slope the dirt or sand downward. Pour water slowly at one end. What happens to the sand or dirt? What would happen if a tremendous amount of water were poured down all at once?

† Do the above activity but simulate a town in the sand or dirt and pour a bucket of water at one time over the "town." What happened? What would happen once the water dissipated? Was anything rapidly buried?

† Use a family-safe search engine and type in the words "stalagmite experiment," or find one in a science resource or experiment book. Find one you would like to create. Be careful with any you choose. These are very delicate experiments and you must follow the directions carefully. Choose the location where you would like your experiment, and make sure you do not touch or move the object while the rocks are growing. Have fun!

Geography/History
K-3

† Observe a globe and notice the differences between the landforms and the waters. Notice the way the earth tilts. Note the large expanse of the ocean and how small the land mass is compared to the waters.

† Observe the shapes of the continents on a world map. Do you think they could have fit together once? Trace a small world map (or find a picture) and cut out the pieces of the continents. Try to put them together. Notice the way they fit. Scientists theorize that at one time the continents were one large land mass.

† Organize the continents from biggest to smallest. Learn the names of the continents.

† Draw a map of the terrain from a nature walk. Note landforms, rivers, streams, oceans, etc. What do you notice about the areas where water stands? Note this in a nature diary. On your map include a legend showing landforms, water, trees, and other important items.

† Learn the compass directions (north, south, east, west). Use these to play the "direction game." Hide an object, and give children directions, such as "Take two steps to the west; turn to the north and take four steps; turn east and take eight steps." Have them look for the object. Variation: have children use a compass.

† Read Genesis 1. Make a three-dimensional model of the "young earth." Use recyclable materials where possible.

† Study a topographical map of the United States of America. Point out highlands, lowlands, mountains, lakes, rivers, etc. Find your state and place a star on it.

† Find the location on a map of the place where Noah's Ark came to a rest (Mt. Ararat). This is also believed to be one of the areas of the earliest civilizations of man.

† Look at a world map, an atlas, or a globe. Ask the children where they think the Garden of Eden might have been. Research where early people lived.

† Look at a world map and locate the places of the earliest civilizations. Color code these places. Notice most civilizations flourished near water. Discuss this and why it was so important.

† The earliest traces of civilization agreed upon by both evolutionists and Creationists are in the Middle East a few thousand years ago. This fits into the Biblical model very nicely. Following the Flood, each tribe migrated around the world as soon as it could. Within a few generations each developed into its own civilization. The descendants are believed to be

from Ham, Shem, and Japheth, Noah's three sons. Locate the area known as the Fertile Crescent and shade in the area on a blank map.

† Research stories of how the world came to be from other cultures such as the American Indians. Compare these to the Genesis account. Do an oral report. What do these cultures have in common? (A flood story.)

† Explain why it would be more than a coincidence for many cultures to have similar Flood stories. Reread Genesis 6-7 and relate this to the oral traditions passed on by other cultures.

† Look at the orderliness of the events of the heavens. What historical events can be tracked in the sky? (Comets, eclipses, etc.)

† Directions help us to locate places quickly. Identify a specific location, within your home or outdoors. With this in mind, blindfold a child and have them reach this destination giving them only directions such as: go three steps to the north, take one step west, now two south, etc. Make sure you review directions before they begin and always have them facing north when they start. This game can be used with many variations and is a great way to learn directions in a fun and non-threatening manner.

† One variation of the above game is to play this with older and younger children. Take turns with the older children giving the younger children the directions. My children love to play this when Mom is blindfolded! This game also teaches trust. You must trust others to direct you in a way that is not harmful (not leading you astray or into a tree!). There is also a parallel in trusting as Noah did, that God had a plan for his life (and ours), and it takes believing and following Him.

† Maps are drawn to scale. Draw a map the size of a sheet of paper or larger. Use your yard or neighborhood. At the bottom of the map, write 1 inch = 10 feet. Figure out the distances on the map using the scale.

† Use a children's atlas containing geographic terminology. Learn terms such as island, basin, sea, stream, river, atoll, etc.—perhaps one per week. Review the terms learned regularly. In this way you may build a very large vocabulary.

† Niagara Falls is eroding at a rate that can be measured (see Teaching Outline Section IV under Evidence for a Young Earth). Find this famous landmark on a map containing North America. Discuss other famous landmarks.

† A premise of evolution is that there are physical changes over time. Discuss time from a historical perspective. Explain a timeline using baby pictures of your child (or show pictures from an album...unless your photos are in a shoebox as are mine). Create a timeline from

birth to your child's current age. Explain how the child changed, but is still a child.

✝ Explain how evolutionary claims of changes over time are radical and unsubstantiated.

✝ A variation of the above activity is to show animals in stages of infancy and as they grow. Explain that animals are still animals even as they mature.

Art and Music
K-3

Art

† God created the sky on the second day. Read Genesis 1:6-8. Explain that sometimes you can discern shapes in the clouds, and see what they can find. Using blue construction paper, glue, and cotton balls, have the children observe the sky and make their own clouds. (A science-related activity would be to teach the different types of clouds.)

† Do a salt painting. Mix 1/2 cup of liquid starch, 2 cups of salt, and 1 cup of water. Color different portions of this mixture with water-based tempera paint powder or food coloring. (Remember that food coloring stains!) Use a heavyweight paper and your salt paint to paint a picture of creation. Your picture will sparkle when it is dry. Variation: use black poster paper or other colors for a neat effect. Create a stormy flood scene or Creation scene.

† Use various sizes of dry beans to create a picture. Glue the beans on the paper and draw designs, or use the beans to create a mosaic. It may be helpful to color in the picture before gluing.

† Make a vegetable print. Using a potato cut in half, carefully cut out a pattern and stamp on brown grocery bags. Crumble up the grocery bags to give texture before stamping. This may be used to wrap gifts. Tie with pretty ribbons or bows.

† Use pipe cleaners to make different types of trees. Some are round, some are triangular, and some look like Christmas trees. A variation on this is to go on a nature walk and collect leaves from various trees. Using the pipe cleaner, create a tree trunk, or draw on a sheet of paper, then glue pipe cleaner and the leaves on the trunk.

† Make Noah's Ark animals out of dough. Use one of the dough recipes on page 142. Use cookie cutter shapes to cut out the dough and allow to air dry or bake.

† Create a snack necklace to take on a nature walk! Use 1 cup of round cereal with a hole in the middle (whatever assortment you wish), a roll of flavored circle candies, etc. Use a shoestring (preferably new) and thread the snack items onto it. Tie and snack as you walk through God's beautiful world.

† Draw or find clip art to depict the days of Creation and create a mobile. Use a wire hanger and hang the various scenes with fishing line or fine thread.

† Fold a piece of paper in half lengthwise and cut it along the fold. Fold one of the strips in half, then in half again. The more folds you make, the smaller your object will be. Draw an object such as a star on the top half of the folded piece of paper. Cut out the star but leave the points on the fold attached. Unfold the paper, and you have a chain.

✝ String letter beads to create a necklace or bracelet using words such as God's Creation, Noah's Ark, or any of the words from this study.

Music

✝ Use various instruments (make your own!) and beat out the sounds of Creation or the Flood (waves crashing, wind blowing, etc.). Use your imagination and stage a Creation performance!

✝ Take two paper plates and some beans and create a percussion instrument. Place a handful of dried beans on one of the plates, glue around the plate's edges, and place the other plate on top. Wait until the glue dries, and you have a tambourine to use as you sing. Experiment with different amounts of dried beans to vary the sounds.

✝ Make different animal sounds. Record them onto a cassette tape and let others guess what kind of animals they are. You can add them to a language arts story or write a new story to go with them.

✝ Play the scale (or hum it). Notice how perfectly the notes are organized.

✝ Use various instruments to perform the above activity. What happens if you play the instrument in a way that it was not designed to be played? Discuss this in relation to the perfection and orderliness of God's Creation.

✝ Listen to various pieces of classical music—which do you think would be playing at the time of Creation if God had chosen to have background music?

✝ Study the orchestra. The term "orchestra" was used in ancient Greek times to describe an area of open-air theater where dancing and singing took place during the performance of a play. Study today's orchestra and the major instruments used. If possible, go to a performance.

✝ Bach and Handel are two well-known composers. Listen to their music. What instruments are used in their most famous compositions? Compare the way orchestras were set up in their day (1600s) and today.

✝ Use eight equal-size glasses to make the sounds of the scale. Line them up and fill them with different amounts of water, slowly increasing the amount in each. Lightly tap on the side to produce a note. Take out or add water to each one to fine-tune your scale. How did you do? A normal scale consists of whole steps and half steps used in the following order: starting note-whole-whole-half-whole-whole-whole-half to produce an octave.

Creation Science Outline
4-8

Objective: To study Creation through observation, comparison, research, and experiments.

I. Days of Creation
    A. Day equals twenty-four-hour time period — Hebrew meaning of word *Yom*
    B. Day One — Light and dark
    C. Day Two — Waters above and waters below
        1. Water vapor canopy
        2. Increased atmospheric pressure — larger plants and animals
        3. Shielded from harmful radiation — longer life span
           (see timeline chart on page vi)
        4. Tropical environment worldwide and no storms
        5. Fountains of the great deep — waters below
    D. Day Three — Dry land and plants
    E. Day Four — Sun, moon, and stars
        1. Light before sun
        2. Stars for signs and to mark the seasons, days, years
    F. Day Five — Fish and birds
    G. Day Six — All other animals and Man

II. Flood Geology and Noah's Ark
    A. Ark designed by God — dimensions and capacity
    B. Fountains of the great deep burst forth — Gen. 7:11
    C. Most geological formations we see were formed during the year-long Flood or soon after (the Grand Canyon)
    D. Sediments and fossils deposited by water (aquatic) on every mountain top
    E. Earth's axis tilts
        1. We now have seasons
        2. Polar ice caps form — Ice Age
    F. Evidence for worldwide Flood — flood interpretation fits what is observed
        1. Fossil fish found in swimming position and fossil insects found in flight
        2. Preservation only possible by rapid burial
        3. Submarine canyons cut by receding water — Guyots
        4. Continental sprint and sea floor spreading

III. Evidence for a Young Earth
    A. Radiometric age dating based on false assumptions
        1. A 170-year-old volcanic eruption misdated 160 million to 3 billion years
        2. Problems with carbon dating
    B. The young island that looks old
    C. Erosion — not enough sediment accumulation in ocean basins if earth is old
    D. Stalactites — formed in building basements in fifty years (not millions)
    E. Sun is young
    F. Moon is receding
    G. Number of comets

IV. Big Bang Theory
    A. Lack of evidence to support theory; based on "faith"
    B. Everything came from nothing and then exploded (chaos not order)
    C. Requires tremendous energy at the beginning — no one knows where this energy came from.
    D. Big Bang Problems

V. Entropy
    A. Conservation of energy — Thermodynamics
    B. Everything seeks a simpler state of being (hot things cool down, metal rusts)

VI. Darwin's Theory Is False
    A. Small changes evolved over long periods of time (macroevolutionary steps)
    B. Darwin said any new changes must be beneficial
    C. Dog breeders always get a dog
    D. Natural selection would have eliminated mutation and abnormalities

VII. DNA, Protein, Amino Acids, and Sugars
    A. Molecules in nature are either left-handed or right-handed. Living organisms require only left-handed molecules and can only combine with purely right-handed sugar molecules.
    B. The probability that these would form by "random chance" is zero
    C. DNA is made using proteins (enzymes); proteins are the building blocks of life which are coded by DNA; which came first? Enigma for evolutionists.

VIII. The Fossil Record
    A. No evidence of any transitional fossils
    B. Stasis — animals stay the same (according to their kind)
    C. Extinction — disappearance of an animal from the fossil record
    D. No evidence of transition from invertebrate to vertebrate or fish to amphibian
    E. Fossil creatures look identical to those of today

IX. False "Ape-Man" Links and Deliberate Hoaxes and Bad Science
    A. Neanderthal Man — new information
    B. Piltdown Man — ape jaw with filed-down teeth and stained to look old
    C. Lucy — measurements taken from crushed bones but used for precise calculations (very bad science)
    D. Java Man — contemporaneous with other hominids
    E. Nebraska Man — an entire family dreamed up and drawn from nothing more than a pig's tooth.
    F. *Australopithecus* — extinct form of ape — name means "southern ape." Lucy was one of these.

X. What Scientists Believe Is Always Changing
    A. Earth is center of solar system
    B. Flies and rats come from garbage
    C. Maggots come from meat
    D. Spontaneous generation — disproved by Louis Pasteur, who stated, "Life always comes from life." Law of Biogenesis

XI. Other Facts
- A. Mount St. Helens — proof of rapid and massive erosion and deposition
- B. Galaxy clusters — if universe were very old, the galaxies should have dispersed
- C. Polystrate fossils — evidence of very rapid deposition of sediments
- D. Flow rate of basalt — if the moon were old, the craters would have smoothed out instead of maintaining sharp edges.

Lesson Plans

Subject Date:	Monday	Tuesday	Wednesday	Thursday	Friday
Bible/Religion Studies	Gen. 1:1-5		Gen. 1:6-8		Gen. 1:9-13
Creation Teaching Outline Timeline chart page vi	I. A-B Days of Creation— Day One		I. C Day Two		I. D Day Three
Reading Selection	Light and dark		Water		Land and plants
Language Arts	Assign ten words from list	Define and write words in sentences	Choose grammar activity	Word meaning bank	Read news for science articles; add vocabulary words to list
Math Reinforcement	Metric system		Make a metric conversion chart		Study area of yard, home and map out
Science Activities and Experiments Days of Creation 1-3	Make vapor canopy	Light wave experiment; magnifying glass and sun's rays	Create rain	Remove oxygen from the air	Grow algae or another plant
Geography/History World Map or Globe	Map skills: study geographical terms	Become familiar with a globe and atlas.	Hypothesize where the Garden of Eden might be located; find on map	Difference between geologists and Creation geologists	Review geographical terms
Art/Music	Stained glass picture	Creation music tape	Finish stain glass picture	Use various instruments; play scales	TS

CR= Creation Resource   TS= Teacher Selection

Lesson Plans

Subject Date:	Monday	Tuesday	Wednesday	Thursday	Friday
Bible/Religion Studies	Gen. 1:14-19	Gen. 1:20-27	Gen. 1:24-31	Gen. 2:1-25	TS
Creation Teaching Outline	I. E Day Four	I. F Day Five	I. G Day Six	God rested	
Reading Selection	Sun, moon, and stars	Birds and fish	All other animals and man	CR	CR
Language Arts	Assign 10 words	Dictionary drill	Use paragraph from Genesis for dictation	Write Creation story in own words	TS
Math Reinforcement	Research calendar system	TS	Ark's dimension activity	TS	Math shortcuts
Science Activities and Experiments Days of Creation 4-6	Make spiral galaxy; comet impacts	Study variations within species	Optical illusion activity	Sound waves and hearing	Observe wood burning
Geography/History World Map or Globe	Study continental sprint	Map world-wide bird migration patterns	Study physical geography and terms	Study human geography	TS
Art/Music	Keep a nature diary and continue to add to it	Use different instruments to simulate nature sounds	Illustrate creation story	TS	TS

CR= Creation Resource   TS= Teacher Selection

Lesson Plans

Week 3 — Flood Geology
4-8

Subject / Date:	Monday	Tuesday	Wednesday	Thursday	Friday
Bible/Religion Studies	Gen. 6:11-21	Gen. 7:11-12	TS	TS	Gen. 7:17-24
Creation Teaching Outline	II. A-B	II. C	II. D.	II. E.	II. F.
Reading Selection	Ark design	Fountains of the deep	Sediments	Earth's axis and tilt	Evidence for worldwide flood
Language Arts	Assign ten words from list	Dictionary drill	Play "What am I?"	Word origins: choose 5-10 words	Write nature poem
Math Reinforcement	Trade after the Flood	TS	Highest mountains	TS	Early men of Bible
Science Activities and Experiments Flood	Create rain	Remove oxygen from the air	Air pressure	Demonstrate porosity	Sedimentation experiment
Geography/History World Map or Globe	Map terrain of nature site, yard, or playground area. Use scale		Study and map (animal) paleontological finds		Study the history of the first kings
Art/Music		Make sand clay and sculpt	Create own music, sounds of nature	Create nature abstract	

CR= Creation Resource

TS= Teacher Selection

Lesson Plans

Week 4—Evidence For Young Earth
4-8

Subject Date:	Monday	Tuesday	Wednesday	Thursday	Friday
Bible/Religion Studies	1 Samuel 2:8 Psalm 102: 25 Prov. 8:27-29	Job 9:9 Job 38: 31-33 Isa. 13:10	TS	Job 11:6 Psalm 103:24 Prov. 2:10-11	CR
Creation Teaching Outline	III. A-C	III. D-G	IV. A-D	V.	VI.
Reading Selection	Radiometric dating; human remains	Stalactites, sun, moon, comets	Big Bang Theory	Entropy	DNA
Language Arts	Assign 10 words from list	Word meaning bank or index cards	Speech refuting evolution	Decide whether statements are true or false	Interview "Darwin"
Math Reinforcement	Study scientific notation		List gases in the atmosphere		How does understand-ing math tie into science?
Science Activities and Experiments III—VI	Study DNA	Stalactite experiment	Big Bang activity	Entropy experiment	Study Darwin's false hypothesis
Geography/History World Map or Globe	Map where "cave man" dwellings have been found	Research areas where caves are prevalent; study famous caves.	Compass skills	TS	Read infor-mation about the island of Galapagos
Art/Music	Do "cave" art	Soap carving		Study famous composers	

CR= Creation Resource

TS= Teacher Selection

Lesson Plans

Week 5 — DNA, Fossil Record
4-8

Subject Date:	Monday	Tuesday	Wednesday	Thursday	Friday
Bible/Religion Studies	Hebrews 11:1-3	Jer. 1:5	TS	Psalm 104	TS
Creation Teaching Outline	VII. A	VII. B—C	VIII. A—B	VIII. C—D	VIII. E
Reading Selection	Molecules	Probability, proteins	No transitional fossils; stasis	Extinction; lack of evidence	Fossil critters
Language Arts	Review and assign remainder of words	Play the game "What am I?"	Write a story about going in search of Noah's ark.	List Creation "facts"	Stage a Creation debate
Math Reinforcement	Fractals	Random chance	Add up ages of early Biblical men	Learn math shortcuts	Make up math short-cuts
Science Activities and Experiments DNA, Fossil record	Make a tongue map	Darwin's black box activity	Research how scientists dated the earth	Optical illusions	Make a fossil print
Geography/History World Map or Globe	Compare physical geography to human geography	Where is Mt. Ararat and why is this significant?	Map and record the where the earliest traces of human civilization have been found	Research information pertaining to ancient remains found at bottom of Mt. Ararat	Expeditions to find fossils are many; map some locations.
Art/Music	Make a stained glass picture	What is the layout of the orchestra?	Do a yarn picture	Talent and music	Frame or use fossil print for art project

CR= Creation Resource

TS= Teacher Selection

Lesson Plans

Week 6 *False Concepts Changing Science*
4-8

Subject / Date:	Monday	Tuesday	Wednesday	Thursday	Friday
Bible/Religion Studies	Col. 2:5 1 Cor. 14:40	TS	1 Tim. 6:20-21	TS	2 Tim 1:6-10
Creation Teaching Outline	IX. A-C	IX. D-F	X.	XI. A-B	XI. C-D
Reading Selection	Hoaxes	Bad science	What scientists believe is always changing	Mt. St. Helens; galaxy clusters	Other facts
Language Arts	Review vocabulary	Write an editorial for your local newspaper about Creation	Play bingo with vocabulary words	Write a research paper at least 5 pages long on any Creation topic	Research survival of the fittest and write a report
Math Reinforcement	Orderliness of mathematics		Fibonacci numbers		Research Fibonacci and write a report
Science Activities and Experiments False Concepts; Changing Science	Blindfold activity	Magnifying glass and nature	Measure the atmosphere	Examine the night sky	Stage your own "creation" demonstration
Geography/History World Map or Globe	Where have the "hoaxes" of evolution been found? Map these.	Study Ernst Haeckel; write about his life	The 1700-1800's was an amazing time of scientific growth. Study this time period	Find Mt. St. Helens on a map; study the before and after	Find Temple of Amen-Ra on map; research
Art/Music	Create an art montage using nature finds	Add to your nature diary	Study Beethoven's Pastoral Symphony		Use geometric shapes to create a picture

CR= Creation Resource   TS= Teacher Selection

Reading List
4-8

*These Christian books may be difficult to find in the library. Use the list of additional resources on page 140 to find these highly recommended titles.

Read Aloud

The Amazing Story of Creation by Duane Gish (Master Books, 1990, 112 pages). This is a wonderful book the whole family will enjoy. Beautifully illustrated.

Bone of Contention is Evolution True? by Sylvia Baker, M.Sc. (Answers in Genesis, 1980, 2001, 35 pages). A magazine-style overview about how evolution has taken over the minds of educators, what fossils prove, genetics, the young earth, and the truth about the history of man. Very interesting reading.

Dinosaurs, The Lost World, & You by John D. Morris, Ph.D. (Master Books, 1999, 48 pages). Clearly explains where dinosaurs fit into the Bible account of Creation.

It Just Couldn't Happen: Fascinating Facts About God's World by Lawrence O. Richards. (Word, Inc., 1989, 191 pages). Biblical answers to difficult questions kids ask about evolution and the world. A great resource.

Origins: Creation or Evolution? by Richard Bliss (Master Books, 1988, 76 pages). Wonderfully illustrated. This is a good reference book with demonstrations of how observable science fits the Creation model rather than the evolution model.

Science and the Bible by Dr. Donald B. DeYoung (Baker Books, 1994, 110 pages). Demonstrations of the laws of nature and Biblical principles that can be done at home with household items and without much preparation time.

Unlocking the Mysteries of Creation by Dennis Petersen (Creation Research Foundation, 1986, revised 2002, 205 pages). This is a great book to get you hooked on the excitement of Creation. Unravel the puzzles of the past through a fascinating study of science and Bible history! Creation knowledge comes alive in this mini-encyclopedia.

Independent Reading

Adam and His Kin by Ruth Beechick (Arrow Press, 1990, 176 pages). Enjoyable fiction that blends Biblical accounts, scientific evidence, archaeological findings, and ancient traditions in a Creation-to-Abram story about real people.

Dinosaurs by Design by Duane Gish (Master Books, 1992, 88 pages). Christian answer to *Jurassic Park*. Are there dinosaurs in the Bible, how are they related to Noah's Flood, what really happened to them, and other questions.

Fossils, Frogs, Fish, and Friends by Kenneth Ernst (Master Books, 1984, 28 pages). Two friends discuss their fascination with the fossil record and the Flood.

The Great Dinosaur Mystery and the Bible by Paul Taylor (Master Books, 1989, 61 pages). Answers questions about fossil clues, where dinosaurs came from, how they became extinct, and many others.

Life in the Great Ice Age by Michael and Beverly Oard (Creation Life Publishers, 1993, 72 pages). Part One is a fictional account of how Noah's descendants got along in the world after the Flood. Spend the summer with a boy and his family as they encounter saber-toothed tigers, cave bears, and woolly mammoths. Part Two explains the scientific reasons for the Ice Age.

The Magic School Bus Inside the Earth by Joanna Cole (Scholastic, Inc., 1987, 40 pages). Fictional book dealing with the inner earth. Written for younger children, but vocabulary discussed is fine for 4th-6th grades.

Noah's Ark and the Ararat Adventure by John Morris (Master Books, 1994, 64 pages). A pleasure to read. Tells the truth about Noah's Ark. Up-to-date information on the latest clues as to the location of Noah's Ark on Mt. Ararat. Contains personal photos from Dr. Morris's real-life search for Noah's Ark.

Resources

Genesis for Kids: Science Experiments That Show God's Power in Creation! by Doug Lambier and Robert Stevenson (Tommy Nelson, 1997, 160 pages). Experiments dealing with light, air and water, land, plants and the sea, the sun, moon, the birds and the fish, animals and people.

How Nature Works by David Burnie (Dorling Kindersley, 1991, 192 pages). While several activities deal with evolution (our teaching outline will combat any questions you may have!) still, this book has very good experiments dealing with Nature.

How Science Works by Judith Hann (Dorling Kindersley, 1991, 192 pages). Many experiments dealing with light and sound, matter, energy, air and water, electricity, etc. that fit in perfectly with the Creation week!

How the Earth Works by John Farndon (Dorling Kindersley, 1991, 192 pages). For a great book with earth science experiments, this one fits the bill. Beautiful color photos throughout and easy-to-perform experiments.

Streams of Civilization, Volume One by Albert Hyma and Mary Stanton (Creation-Life Publishers, 1992, 410 pages). A very good and comprehensive romp through history from the dawn of the world to A.D.1294! This book is written from a Creationist perspective and was actually sponsored by the Institute for Creation Research. A must-have.

Vocabulary/Spelling List
4-8

	universe		relativity
	density		creation
	firmament		radiometric dating
	invertebrates		vertebrates
	Greenhouse Effect		environment
	fossil record		Peleg
	sedimentary		evolution
	evolutionists		creationists
	vapor canopy		fountains of the great deep
	atmospheric pressure		continental drift
	radiation		aquatic
	assumptions		stalactites
	stalagmites		growth rates
	population		evidence
	beneficial		molecule
	transitional		stasis
	extinction		geologist
	astronomer		galaxy clusters
	deposition		sedimentation
	erosion		speed of light
	light year		polystrate

Vocabulary/Spelling/Grammar

4-8

Use the vocabulary and spelling words interchangeably in the following activities.

Have children look up the vocabulary words in a dictionary or use an online source. Use the words in sentences showing their meaning. Use the sentences the children have written to study the parts of speech.

† Learn the parts of speech. Use the children's sentences to do the following activity:
Underline nouns once.
Underline verbs twice.
Put a squiggly line under the adjectives.
Put two squiggly lines under the adverbs.
Put a box around the prepositions.
Circle a pronoun and put a "p" above it.
(Continue this activity with parts of speech you are studying.)

† Use colored pencils or markers in the above grammar activity, assigning a color to a part of speech.

† Choose the "best" sentences and have the children practice their handwriting. Have the children highlight the adjectives and use a thesaurus to find different words to replace the adjectives.

† Make a word meaning bank. This can be a personal bank of words the child has difficulty learning. Use 3-by-5-inch index cards. Keep them in alphabetical order. Put the word on the front and the definition on the back. Decorate a container for the word bank.

† Have a dictionary drill. Give the children a list of five words and have them race against the clock. Time how long it takes them to find each word. Do this several times with different words (or the same ones). They should try to beat their previous time.

† Look in the newspaper for scientific articles dealing with astronomy, oceanography, or weather. Use these articles to find their vocabulary words (or add to their list).

† Make a crossword or word-find puzzle using the vocabulary words.

† Scramble the vocabulary words. Have the children unscramble them.

† Take one vocabulary word and write it on a sheet of paper omitting the vowels. See if your student can guess the word. Do this with as many of the words as you wish. This is an easy and painless way to become familiar with the pronunciation of the words.

† Have the children write riddles for the vocabulary words. Try to guess the words. Use this in a game or create a card game such as "go fish" using the words.

† Find the word origins of a few of the words. What are their countries of origin? Locate the countries on the world map. Is there a story behind any of the words? Try to find the words in the encyclopedia. You may want to use an online source or do a key word search (online). How many words have Greek or Latin roots? Learn why Greek and Latin were widely spoken in countries around the Mediterranean Sea.

† Play "What am I?" with the vocabulary words. For example, "I am larger than the earth, the sun and all the planets, I consist of other solar systems, what am I?" (Answer: universe)

† Assign a word of the day. Before the unit begins make a calendar (placing the day of the week on each card). You may want to use index cards for this activity. Place one vocabulary word on each day. You may borrow from the vocabulary lists from K-3 and 9-12 for this activity. Make use of this word for the day. See who can use the word in context the most times during the day. This is a great way to build your vocabulary.

† Use the vocabulary words to make bingo cards. Use grids of twenty-five. Place five grids across and five grids down. Leave the middle square blank. Insert various words in each grid, leaving a middle space blank and marking it free (if you desire). Play bingo!

Language Arts Ideas
4-8

† Begin an open-ended story. Example: " While taking my sheep to drink from the River Tigris, I spotted a huge footprint. Could it be a dragon (dinosaur) print? I had not seen any recently. Just then I heard a shout in the distance. Looking, I saw the dreaded dragon chasing a band of travelers. Without hesitation I ran in their direction. I knew just what to do...."

† Try different variations of the open-ended story. The creature can be whatever animal you are currently studying. This activity can be done orally in a group with children of different ages.

† Give a paragraph from Genesis as dictation. Have children read the passage first to become familiar with the words. Have younger children copy the paragraph before you begin dictating.

† Research Newton or Kepler. Have children write a paper of no more than 250 words telling about the most notable accomplishments of one of them. Do a rough draft first, double-spaced. They should correct their own spelling, punctuation, etc. If there are other children, have them trade papers and correct each other's, or work together. Rewrite the finished product single-spaced. If you have access to a typewriter or computer, have them type their work.

† Pretend you are doing an interview with Charles Darwin. Ask him questions such as, "What proof do you have that anything evolved?" "Why don't you believe that God created the world?" Continue along this line. Tape this interview!

† Decide whether statements are fact or opinion. Read various statements made in any book found in the library dealing with the earth, astronomy, geology, etc. Decide whether the statements are true or false. For example, in geology there are many claims that the formation of fossils took many millions of years. Use critical thinking skills to determine if such claims are logical!

† Using different forms, write a poem about Creation, evidence for a young earth, fossils, etc.

† Write both sides of a debate, pro and con, about Creation vs. evolution. Variation: have children hold an impromptu debate.

† List several Creation facts and use these in a debate with an evolutionist.

† Pretend evolutionists say they found the Missing Link. What would this mean to Creation scientists and to evolutionists? Write a fictional story of about 800-1000 words.

† If you lived at the time of Peleg, when God confused the languages at the tower of Babel, how would you have felt? Write a short story or play depicting the reactions of the people once their language was confused. Variation on this activity: if your family had gathered together once the languages had been confused, describe where you would go and what you would do for survival. Think of this happening today. Would you be able to survive without all the modern conveniences?

† You are the editor of the *Morning Glory Gazette,* and the latest news is that someone named Noah is building an Ark at the commission of God. The year is 2004. What happens?

† Discuss the temptation in the garden. Did Eve really know who the serpent was? Where was Adam when she was tempted? Write a short one-scene play depicting this. Act this out or use hand puppets. Point out that God gave us free will and we are not puppets.

† Pretend you were an animal in the garden of Eden observing what transpired between Adam, Eve, and the serpent. Use hand puppets to act out the scene. You may want to do this with a group of children, with an adult using the hand puppet. The puppeteer may interact with the audience and ask questions such as, "Oh, no! What do you think Eve should do now?"

† The dinosaurs were a species of animal on the Ark with Noah. Create a short story about the trials of traveling with the dinosaurs. Many believe the dinosaurs were juvenile species. Use internet sources for information (or obtain the book entitled *Noah's Ark: A Feasibility Study* by John Woodmorrappe).

† Do a study of the lineage from Adam and Eve through to Abraham and the twelve tribes of Israel. List them in a flow chart. Use Biblical resources.

† Write a fictional story weaving in Creation details. For example, Christina and Felice Gerwitz have authored the *Truth Seeker's Mystery Series* using the Creation model and specifics about the Creation-Evolution debate. The story captures the reader with an exciting adventure story while the reader learns how to debate creation topics with evolutionists. Try your hand at writing one! First, outline a plot idea. Then write about your characters. Make each of your main characters have personality. One of the easiest ways we have found is to base our characters on traits from people we know. List as many character traits as you can for each person. For example: name, temperament, eye, hair, skin color, stature, favorite books, ice cream, movie, etc. Keep this list handy as you write, as you may want to make changes to the list or use it as a resource. Remember a book is written one chapter at a time. You don't necessarily need to have the details of the conclusion hammered out in advance. Sometimes it changes as the story progresses. Above all, try to weave in some Creationism in your account. (That was after all, the purpose of this assignment!)

Math Reinforcement
4-8

† Learn about the metric system. Why is this form of math used in science?

† Make a conversion table. Convert inches, feet, yards, miles, etc. into metric units. Convert cups, quarts, and gallons to liters, ounces and pounds to kilograms, etc.

† Measure an area such as your yard and map it out. Figure out the total square footage. Figure out the total square footage of lawn space. (Subtract the square footage of your home or building.) Convert all measurements to metric.

† Use a protractor, a ruler, and a compass. What shapes can be made with these items? Design as many separate shapes as you can. Combine the different tools and make shapes. Discuss the usefulness of each tool and the limitations of using it in isolation. (How does this apply to our lives and trying to do things with our own strength?) Variation: use geoboards.

† How does an understanding of mathematics tie into scientific principles? Are scientists good mathematicians?

† How did men trade after the Flood? What did they use for money? Why did they trade? What became valuable for trade? Do we use money the same way today? What is bartering? Set up a bartering system.

† Find the highest mountains and write down their heights. Use combinations of these numbers to add, subtract, multiply, and divide.

† List all the gases found in the atmosphere. Write them in percentages, decimals, and fractions.

† Find the early men of the Bible. Add up their ages. How did Creation scientists come up with the figure of the Earth's age? How did evolutionists come up with the figure of the Earth's age?

† Research the calendar system. How was it first devised? How does the moon correlate to the months? How are the orderliness and consistency of the earth's path around the sun a help?

† Here is a fun exercise that requires a large area such as a park. The Ark's measurements are found in Genesis 6: 300 cubits in length, 50 cubits in breadth (width), and 30 cubits in height. An average cubit is 18 inches. Convert cubits to feet. Use different colored string and stakes to mark out the dimensions of the Ark.

† Calculate the Ark's capacity. There have been feasibility studies, and a book was written on this concept. Try your hand at this and then do some research. How accurate were you?

† Study the growth rate of stalactites and stalagmites. They are said to take millions of years to grow, yet some are growing under the Lincoln Monument in Washington, D.C. Research this phenomenon and calculate a rate factor.

The following activities were adapted and taken from *Math Wizardry for Kids:* (Barrons, 1995). This book is highly recommended.

† God is a God of order. Mathematics is orderly and logical. To prove this, measure a circle. Trace the bottom of a coffee or other round container. Place a dot in the middle of the circle. Draw a straight line horizontally through the dot. This is the diameter. Measure this line and record the number. Use a piece of yarn and place it around the bottom of the coffee can. Make sure the yarn is even all the way around. Cut the yarn where the ends meet. Use a ruler and measure the yarn. Divide the length of the yarn by the length of the diameter of the circle and learn how many diameters there are in the circumference of your circle. (Answer is 3.14159....) This number is known as pi, which the Greeks named for the sixteenth letter of their alphabet. Try this activity measuring various sizes of circles. What is your answer?

† Pi has been studied since ancient times. Pi allows mathematicians to make difficult measurements. While it is useful, it still is a puzzle. Many people want to know the exact measurement of pi, but they have never found the answer. Research this phenomenon. Why do you think man still struggles trying to understand this mystery?

† Fractals are beautiful shapes with mathematical properties that can be measured. For example, frost on a window is a fractal. A fractal is a basic shape that duplicates itself over and over again. Some of the patterns are very complex. Try to observe fractals in nature. Some computer generated fractals are created using mathematical formulas. Research these. Some are truly works of art!

† Leonardo Fibonacci was born in Italy in 1175 and grew up with a fascination for numbers. The system of numbers he brought back from Algeria, where he and his family lived for awhile, was the Hindu-Arabic numerals we still use today. These consist of counting beginning with 0, 1, 2, 3, 4, 5, 6, 7, 8, 9, 10 ... This was different from the Roman numerals used in his day: I, II, III, IV, V, VI, VII, VIII, IX, X.... He discovered a sequence of numbers to explain math in nature. This is called the Fibonacci numbers. Here is his sequence of numbers; see if you can add to this. 1, 1, 2, 3, 5, 8, ... (The next numbers would be 13, 21, 34, 55...) How did you arrive at the solution? Try this out on your family or friends. Give them the first 6 numbers and see if they can arrive at the solution. (Hint: add two adjacent numbers to get the next one in the series.)

† Using Fibonacci numbers, see if you can observe patterns in nature. Slice open a fruit or vegetable such as a cucumber (make slices), tomato, lemon, etc. Count the sections inside the slice. You do not count each individual seed contained within the vegetable or fruit, but

look at the grouping of seeds, that is the sections that lie together. For example a cavity of a cucumber has three sections or groups of seeds, the cavity of a tomato has three, etc. Apply this concept to other plants in nature. Look at pine needle clusters, a sunflower, or a pineapple for examples.

† Mathematical shortcuts save time and are fun. Look at patterns in numbers. Try multiplying a lot of numbers by 11. What do you find? In your answers look for the numbers 12, 13, 14, and 15. Then look in the middle of each answer. What can you add to get that middle answer? Try multiplying numbers by 11 in your head, once you've memorized 11 x 12 of course, and impress your family and friends! Design your own mathematical shortcuts.

† You may want to play with this idea, but it is much better to memorize your mathematical facts! Here how to multiply by 9 using your fingers. Hold your hands, palm sides down before you. Imagine a the number one for your left pinky, all the way to ten for your right pinky. Begin with the problem 9 x 4. Bend down the 4th finger on your left hand. Now this is where it gets tricky. How many fingers are still up to the left of the 4th finger? (3) How many fingers are still up to the right of the 4th finger? (6). The answer is 36. Do all your nine facts and see how accurate this method is. You can teach this to younger children.

Science Activities and Experiments
4-8

A good understanding of the scientific method is a must at this grade level! (Authors' personal bias!) Many good science books talk about the scientific method (see page 59 for an overview). Remember to formulate your question and hypothesis before you begin an experiment! At this age give children flexibility to experiment. If they have an idea of something they want to try, allow them time to experiment. It is helpful if they write out their procedures using scientific method sheets (copy section begins on page 146). In the event that they invent something wonderful, they will be able to duplicate the experiment! **Always use caution when doing any science projects and experiments. Parental supervision is necessary!**

You may wish to set up experiments under the headings of the Creation Week. To do this plan activities and experiments for Light and Dark; Waters Above and Waters Below; Dry Land and Plants; Sun, Moon, and Stars; Birds and Fish; Animals and Man.

Light and Dark

† What is light? Several noted scientists through the years have disagreed about the properties of light. Research this.

† Take turns blindfolding each other and trying to navigate out of a room. How difficult is this to do without light in order to see? Try giving verbal clues to help the blindfolded person. Does this help? Try your own variations of this activity.

† There are many types of light waves. One example is on your television set and in a flashlight. In a very dark room place your hand on the television screen. Using a flashlight make sure every inch of the television is covered in light except the portion where your palm is. Do this for several minutes, making sure your hand does not move. Remove your hand. What do you see?

† Take a magnifying glass outdoors and try to harness the sun's rays to make a fire. Be careful with this activity! What types of items burn quickly? Which took longer? Chart these.

† Demonstrate the necessity of light for living things to grow. Place one plant in the sunlight and another in a dark closet. Compare them every day. What are the results? What does this tell us about the importance of the light that God created?

Waters Above and Waters Below

† There is much dispute over whether there really was a vapor canopy barrier at some point after God created the world. Research this on www.icr.org or www.answersingenesis.org. Compare what they say.

† Study the three properties of matter using water. Which is the most dense?

† What is a vacuum? You can create a demonstration of one with a clear plastic cup (or glass), water, and an index card or other hard paper. Fill a cup with water to the top, then place the index card on top of the filled cup (making sure the paper covers the entire top). Holding the index card against the cup, invert it quickly. Carefully take your hand away from the index card. What happens? Do variations of this experiment with larger cups and larger stiff cards.

† The air that we breathe is mostly made up of oxygen and carbon dioxide. We exhale the carbon dioxide when we breathe. Carbon dioxide may be created by mixing one tablespoon of baking soda with three tablespoons of white vinegar in a bottle. Use this gas to extinguish a candle. You can "pour" out the carbon dioxide. Be creative in your experiment and record your results. Did it work?

† Measure the temperature in the atmosphere. Using a fishing rod and reel, a helium-filled balloon, and an air thermometer, create an experiment to measure the earth's troposphere. Is the temperature warmer on land or above? How much line did you release? Record your results.

† Create rain with the following items: a tea kettle, stove, water, ice cubes, dinner plate, oven mitts. Place a tea kettle full of water on the burner to boil. Once the steam is released, hold the dinner plate with a oven mitt and place several ice cubes on top of the plate, then place the edge of the dish over the steam. What happens? It might be a wise idea to have a tray or large bowl under the dinner plate to catch the "rain."

† Do this activity to remove oxygen from the air. Get some steel wool without soap or anything in it. If it has a protective oily covering, be sure to wash it thoroughly in soapy water and let it dry. Push the steel wool firmly into the bottom of a glass, then turn it upside down into a bowl of water. Observe and record the level of the water inside the glass. (The iron in the steel wool will attract the oxygen and cause it to rust. As more oxygen is changed into iron oxide, the water will be pushed up into the glass, displacing the volume of the oxygen.)

† Air weighs a ton! Did you know that on every square foot of surface, air exerts about a ton of pressure? Prove that air has weight. Obtain several wooden yardsticks from your local hardware store. Place a yardstick on a table so that 6-8 inches sticks out from the edge. Place two sheets of unfolded, flattened newspaper over the part of the yardstick that is on the table. You need to press down on the paper and smooth it out to remove any air from underneath. Do not cover the part that extends out from the table. Now strike the end of the yardstick very hard with your fist or a hammer. (Be careful not to hit anyone else.) Instead of throwing the newspaper up, the yardstick breaks due to the weight of the air! (Moving the

yardstick slowly gives the molecules of air time to move out of the way.)

Dry Land and Plants

† Take turns making up a scavenger hunt of things that may be found on a nature walk. Be creative in your list and include items that can be interpreted in various ways such as: a blade, something containing chlorophyll, a biodegradable object, a non-biodegradable object, something wet, something that doesn't retain water, a living item, something dead, something shiny, a dull item, an item with texture, something pointy, etc.

† Grow algae: There are thousands of algae strains, and many are green due to chlorophyll. Take a clear jar and place water from a pond, lake, or aquarium (one that needs cleaning). Place a plant (any kind of aquatic plant) in the jar, then place the jar near a window that receives sunlight. Examine the jar every day. How long does it take for the algae to grow?

† Demonstrate porosity (the pores or spaces between the grains of rock). Ask the question: Will rocks and water fill two containers in the same way? Find two containers that are the same size. Fill one with rocks and the other with water. Do the rocks fit as nicely as the water does? Why not? See the spaces between the rocks? These are like the microscopic pores in rocks. Now pour some of the water into the container with the rocks. How much water can fit into the spaces? This is like the oil or water found in rock formations beneath the surface of the earth.

† Make a leaf collection. Take samples of leaves in your neighborhood, recording the location where they came from. Name the kind of tree each leaf came from. Examine the leaves under a magnifying lens or microscope and determine how they are alike and how they are different. Make sure you are able to recognize poisonous leaves like poison ivy and poison oak and be sure to avoid them. Press the leaves into a book, and make a nice cover for your leaf collection.

† Plan a family trip to the Grand Canyon (or some other location). Determine the mileage and how many days it will take to get there from your home. Figure out the number of gallons of gas it will take to drive that distance using your car's miles/gallon rate. If you are fortunate enough to visit the Grand Canyon, observe the stratigraphy and consider how Noah's Flood laid down all the layers that you are looking at. Disregard the tour guide's explanation of millions of years. If you can't take a trip to the Grand Canyon, determine the mileage and the gallons and then check out a Grand Canyon movie from your library. If you would like a Creationist perspective of the formation, visit www.icr.org or plan to join them on one of their Grand Canyon tours.

† Demonstrate sedimentation. Take a large jar with a lid and fill it with as many different types of material as you can find such as: dirt, sand, pebbles, rocks, pine needles, shells, or other yard debris. Fill the jar with water and shake it up. Place the jar on a surface where it

will not be disturbed and observe it every hour for a day. Then observe it daily for several days. What did you observe about the layering of the various materials? How long did it take for the material to settle out of the mix? Record your observations on a timetable.

† Entropy is the opposite of order. Demonstrate entropy in action. Build a large sand castle in your back yard or at the beach. Measure and record its dimensions (length, width, and height) every day for a week. What is happening to the sand castle? Does it look as nice as when you first made it? Does it have the same amount of order? Explain why or why not and how this demonstrates the Second Law of Thermodynamics.

† Evolutionists believe it takes millions of years for stalactites and stalagmites to form. They actually take much less time than this. You can make them grow in just a few days with this experiment. You will need to thoroughly wash and rinse 2 pint jars. Put 5 tablespoons of washing soda (sodium carbonate, which can be found in the laundry section of your grocery store) and 1½ cups of hot water into each jar. Stir thoroughly until the soda has completely dissolved. Cut a length of wool, such as yarn, about 18 inches long to be used as a wick. Place the jars on a cookie sheet with a small plate in between to catch the drips. Find the center of the yarn and hold it above the plate. Then put one end of the yarn into each jar. Adjust so that the yarn is above the plate and below the tops of the jars. The solution will begin to drip from the yarn. Watch the stalactite grow. This will take several days. If you leave it long enough you will see a stalagmite grow up from the plate.

Sun, Moon, and Stars

† Demonstrate a spiral galaxy. Take a cup of hot chocolate (be careful of burns!) and use a spoon to stir the contents. Remove the spoon and slowly pour a little bit of milk, half, and half or heavy cream into the center of the coffee. What happens?

† Harness the power of the sun. Although the sun is far away, the warmth of its rays is very powerful. Devise a solar cooker. Line the inside of the shoe box (or other deep box) with heavy aluminum foil, curving it so that it will radiate the heat up. Place a small wire grate inside the box, and put your hamburger or hot dog on the grate. Cover the box with clear wrap and place it in the sun. How long does it take your food to cook? Note: You may wish to check the meat with a food thermometer to insure it is well cooked before you eat it. Variation: try lining the box with foil in different ways to maximize the sun's heat. Cook a variety of foods this way. If you are adventurous try baking a cake in your solar oven.

† Construct a sundial. Search online for "Sundial Experiments" and pick one that suits you.

† Examine the night sky. Take out a blanket and lie outdoors on your back. It takes around thirty minutes for your eyes to adjust to the evening sky. Try to do this in a dark place and do not use a flashlight (if you do, cover it with red transparent clear film). Try to identify the constellations. Indoors, draw the constellations with chalk and black paper.

† The moon is our closest celestial neighbor. How does the moon affect the earth? List these different things.

† Describe why we only see one side of the moon. Do a demonstration to explain this phenomenon. Also, explain where the "light" from the moon comes from.

† The Earth is the third planet from the sun. Why is this the optimum place to be? Explain what would happen if we were closer to the sun, the axis of the earth were tipped more, the Earth rotated less quickly, etc.

† Make a straw rocket. Use an empty dish soap dispenser (with a pop-up lid) or water bottle with a sport top, a straw (two sizes—one needs to fit within the other), and a quarter-size piece of clay or clay dough. Make sure the empty bottle shoots out air when squeezed rapidly. Glue the bottom of the larger of the two straws on the top of bottle. Make sure the air passage is not affected and the air can squirt out of the straw. Allow the straw to dry well. Hot glue works great for this activity. Form the clay into the shape of a small cone and fit it onto the top of the narrow straw. Place this "rocket" into the larger straw. Rapidly squeeze the bottle and watch the rocket shoot out. This demonstrates Isaac Newton's third law of motion: for every action there is an opposite and equal reaction.

† Demonstrate comet impacts. Cover a large cookie sheet with flour, then sprinkle paprika to completely cover the flour. Now stand above the cookie sheet and drop marbles of differing sizes one at a time onto the sheet. Observe the shape of the impact craters formed when the marbles hit the sheet. Notice how the ridge is formed by the flour and the paprika after the marble has impacted the surface.

† According to the Big Bang Theory, how did evolution begin? Create your own "Big Bang" with a balloon and confetti. Stuff confetti into a balloon, then inflate it. (Be careful when blowing into a balloon with tiny particles in it. Don't inhale! **Only an adult should do this!!**) Pop the balloon. Do the pieces of confetti form a piece of paper? Do the pieces of confetti form a distinct pattern? If you did this ten times would the results change? If you did this a million times would the results change? (How do you get order from disorder?) Variation: use Popsicle sticks. See page 60 for another big bang activity.

Birds and Fish

† Study variations with species. How different can birds be? How are they the same? List and characterize at least 20 different species. Do the same thing with fish.

† Not all sea creatures fall into the classification of "fish." Some are mammals. Explain the differences between a fish and a mammal.

✝ Birds have a unique bone structure that allows them to fly. Research and draw this (or use illustrations from books or clip art).

✝ Soak a clean chicken bone in a cup or two of vinegar in a sealed glass jar. Make sure the bone is completely submerged. How long does it take before you can bend the bone? Why does this happen?

✝ Dissect a fish. Use a good book on animal dissections to identify all the parts of a fish. What are some amazing design features that are unique to fish?

✝ Some species of birds and fish are incredibly strange to humans. List some that defy our imagination, for which only seeing is believing.

✝ Make custom bird feeders. Melt some lard and pour it over kitchen scraps like cut-up vegetables, cooked rice, small pieces of bread, oats, and birdseed. Spoon this mixture into small containers, insert a twig for hanging, and let cool. When cooled, roll in more birdseed and hang outside. Observed and record the kinds of birds that visit your feeders. What do the birds like the best? How would you adjust the ingredients in your feeders?

Animals and Man

✝ What is DNA? What came first, DNA or protein?

✝ Do a tongue map. Which area of the tongue tastes sour, bitter, sweet, and salty? Try this activity in a group of children, making sure one is blindfolded. Use diced pieces of fruit, lemon, candy, onions, etc. and touch an area of the tongue of a blindfolded child. Usually smells give the food away, so try to set the items away from the blindfolded child.

✝ Michael J. Behe wrote *Darwin's Black Box* to explain the complexity of micro-organisms, those not seen with the eye. If one item in the perfect design were missing, the organism would not function correctly. Apply this concept to our bodies: how could we function without a limb, eye, etc.? Explain.

✝ We are incredibly made. Each individual is unique, and the pattern of our fingerprints proves this. Rub a soft pencil across a sheet of paper to layer graphite on the surface. Rub your pointer (index) finger over the graphite, then use a piece of tape take your print off the finger, and place the tape on a sheet of paper to make a print. Do this with your other fingers. With a magnifying glass study the prints. What do you see? Compare your prints to those of other people.

✝ Optical illusions are fun, and there are many variations of this. Try a simple one. Roll up a sheet of paper into a tube. Hold the tube up to your right eye and look straight into it. Leave both eyes open and do not move your head. Look at an object in front of you, and as you do this, place your left hand against the tube with your palm facing up. What happens?

† Draw a food pyramid labeling the various groups: carbohydrate, vegetable, protein, dairy, and fat. Plan your menus for a week, being sure to incorporate 5-6 servings of fruits and vegetable each day. Explain the difference between junk food and good food. Help your mom to prepare meals.

† Sound waves and hearing. Sit in a chair blindfolded. Have another student snap his fingers or clap his hands directly in front of, above, and behind you. Try to tell where the sound came from. Now have several students (two or more) sit on the floor around the chair. Have them snap their fingers (or clap if they can't snap) in random order, and point to where you think the sound came from. [In the first activity the sound reached your ears at the same time, and it is sometimes hard to tell where it came from. In the second activity the sound reaches your ears at different times, and your brain (your personal computer) calculates the location of the sound.]

† What is the basis for evolution? What is the basis for Creation? Can either be proved? What is faith? What is evidence? What is science?

† Is there evidence of transitional fossils? Research the term "survival of the fittest." How could a transitional creature survive?

† What is wrong with the fossil record from Darwin's viewpoint?

† Make your own fossil print. Dip an item (rock or shell) into petroleum jelly or oil to coat. Press it into clay and remove. Mix plaster of Paris and pour into the clay mold. Wait until it dries and hardens. Carefully peel off the clay, and you have a fossil print. (In places of high humidity, such as Florida, these things sometimes take a long time to dry!)

† What did Aristotle's model of the universe look like? Make a model of this using two balls, one symbolizing the earth and the other symbolizing the sun.

† How was Copernicus's model of the universe different? Draw a diagram to represent this solar system. What does our solar system look like? What is the difference?

† How are energy and matter related? Observe a piece of wood burning. The material in the wood is changed into heat and light energy, which can be felt and seen.

Geography/History Ideas
4-8

† Become familiar with a globe, an atlas, world maps, and geographical terminology.

† Study the deliberate hoaxes using the Teaching Outline sections IX and XI. In what periods of time did these different hoaxes occur? Make a timeline. Write a comparison of the different scientists such as Ernst Haeckel, Eugene DuBois, or Donald Johanson. (Louis Pasteur is an example of a scientist who had correct thinking.) What were their beliefs? Did any of the scientists believe in a Divine Creator?

† Study continental sprint (or plate tectonics). Use a world map and draw in the rift lines such as the Mid-Atlantic Ridge. How are the new findings confounding evolutionists?

† Pin a map of the world on a bulletin board. Use different colored push pins to label various places where dinosaurs have been found. Use longitude and latitude lines to mark your findings.

† Study the difference between geologists and Creation geologists. Study one Creationist and learn as much as possible about him. Pretend you are interviewing him. What questions would you ask? List the questions and answers.

† Map the terrain from a nature site you have visited. Label your map with a legend showing rock formations and types, ponds, streams, and lakes or any other bodies of water. Note any buildings or other areas of interest. Be sure to label your map with directions (north, south, east, and west).

† Study a topographical map of the United States of America. Label a blank map with the different areas such as mountains, plains, wetlands, oceans, seas, etc.

† There are many great online resources for topographical maps. The USGS (United States Geological Services) has one site that provides wonderful aerial views as well as detailed maps. Do a word search for this site or other similar ones.

† Many paleontological excavations take place all over the world, but often they are right in our own back yard. For example, several bones from a mammoth have been excavated in Arcadia, Florida, which is less than two hours from my home. Many amazing dinosaur finds have taken place in in Colorado and Montana. Map out other excavations taking place all over the United States. Are there any near where you live? If so, try to join the expedition!

† Physical geography contains information about the earth, time zones, climate zones, and physical landform attributes. Human geography contains information about nationality, race, language, religion, government, and culture. Find a human geography map and find the region where the eight main races live: Australian (Aborigines), African, Asian,

Caucasian, Indian, Native American, Melanesian, and Polynesian. (All the tribes can be traced back to our common ancestors, Adam and Eve.)

† Study the history of governments. Using online, library, and Scripture sources, study the very beginning of governments.

† When were the first kings introduced into society? Look at Scripture sources for the first king. Who was this? Look in I Kings.

† Use a compass to find your way home. Map an area at a local park or other wooded area, using only compass readings to find your way back to "start." Give these directions to a group of children (or do this with your family). You may wish to divide the group into two and time how long it takes to complete the task.

† What are the characteristics of the area known as Mesopotamia? Where is this located.? Research the earliest inhabitants. What do you find? Recent archaeology has shown inhabitants in other places—where? (At the base of Mt. Ararat, the mountain where some believe Noah's Ark rests.)

† Research Mt. Ararat, its location, and the culture of today. Now research expeditions that have gone to this locale in an attempt to find Noah's Ark. Research this information on Creation websites or in libraries. As yet the expeditions haven't been successful; why is this?

† Environmental issues are a great concern to many people in the world, yet some take the position to an extreme. Man was given dominion over the world, yet this doesn't mean we should abuse our natural resources. Research and explain the main issues concerning environmentalists and why we, as Christians, should take heed, yet be concerned when environment becomes a type of god. Your focus may be on the issues of water, air, animals, or land use.

† Transportation and communication are two ways in which we share resources and information with our fellow man. Explain what the situation was like in the world back in Noah's day. How might news that Noah was building an Ark reach the masses of people in his day?

† Research the migration paths of birds. What are their summer and winter feeding grounds? What states do they cross in the migratory route? Draw a map of the route you studied.

† Study Mt. St. Helens and locate it on a map. What was the environment like pre-volcano and post-volcano? What is the terrain like today? Why does this area make a compelling case for Creationists?

† Find the Temple of Amen-Ra on a map. Research this temple and explain its significance. What are some archeological marvels that cannot be explained by modern science? Research these. If God created man intelligent is it any wonder that man was able to accomplish much?

† Study Ernst Haeckel and write about his life and discoveries. Were they well received in his day?

† The 1700s and the 1800s were a time of an explosion of scientific growth and amazing inventions and discoveries. Study this period of time and list at least twenty discoveries that changed our world.

† On a map, graph some of the places where evolution "hoaxes" are said to be found. Are these in particular geographical locations? Compare these to recent finds. Where are the most amazing "finds" being hailed from today? (Try researching this online.) Why is this? What type of responsibility do modern scientists have? (To follow true scientific principles.) Is this being fulfilled?

† Study the Grand Canyon. Why is this such a geographical monument? Where is it located? How many visitors travel there each year?

Art/Music Ideas
4-8

Art

† Make a stained glass picture. You will need eggshell, food coloring, vinegar, and liquid white glue. Wash pieces of eggshell and allow to dry. Save eggshell in the freezer until you have enough accumulated for this activity. Each color will need ½ cup of water, ½ teaspoon of vinegar, and 2-3 drops of food coloring. Set up several bowls of color. Crush eggshells and soak in different color dyes for 5-10 minutes. Lay colored shells on wax paper or paper towels to dry. Glue the shells to construction paper. Make a picture of Noah's Ark once it had landed on dry land!

† Make a yarn picture. Have children take a favorite design or artistic scribble to be used for the picture. Cut different lengths of yarn. Dip colored yarn in liquid white glue. Arrange in a pattern on wax paper, overlapping the yarn as you make the design. Allow this to dry. Peel off the wax paper and hang the picture.

† Make sand clay. Cook 1 cup of cornstarch, 2 cups of sifted sand, and 1½ cups of cold water on medium heat, stirring constantly, until the mixture is very thick and holds its shape. Put mixture on a plate and cover with a damp cloth until cool enough to knead. Knead well. Store in an airtight container. Use this clay to make sand castles—a great rainy day activity! Use Popsicle sticks, rulers, and other items to add straight ends, and decorate.

† Keep a nature diary with pictures or photographs. Don't forget to label, date, and note the location. If you have a digital camera, use it to create a book on the computer. Import your pictures and write interesting captions.

† Use objects found in nature to create an abstract picture. Use your imagination; for example, use large leaves and cut out silhouettes of various objects such as buildings, mountains, or streams. Use pine needles to make grass, glue sand to make a path, etc.

† Research the dimensions of Noah's Ark. Draw a picture of Noah's Ark (Variation: using mathematics draw the picture to scale.)

† Soap carving is similar to sculptures—that is, taking a solid object and "releasing" the art within. Sculpting was a popular form of art at the time of the Renaissance. Many masterpieces with religious themes were created out of stone and marble. Use a paring knife or other sharp whittling tool to carve out an object of your choice from a soap bar. If you use a very soft soap be careful; it breaks easily. Try using harder soaps.

† Construct night-light lanterns from empty tin cans. Remove the label and use permanent marker to make dots or a pattern where you would want the holes to appear. Place water in the can and freeze for at least 24 hours. Place the can on its side on a folded towel, then

hammer in assorted nails to pierce through the pattern of dots drawn. Hammer the nails in just far enough to pierce the metal. When done, place the cans in the sink to drain out the water and dry. Warning: the inside of the can will have jagged edges; take care when placing a small tea candle at the bottom. These can be spray painted on the outside and used for outdoor decorations or to light a path during the holiday season. Use the plastic cap of the can to place on top and store when not in use.

† Make a montage. Look at a landscape and instead of seeing a tree, notice the shape of the trunk as a rectangle and the foliage as a circle. Carry this idea over to the other items in nature and create a montage of shapes depicting a landscape or still life. Use paint or cut out shapes for this activity. Variation: you may use old photos that are going to be tossed out or shots you don't like, and cut out segments of these pictures. Make a montage by gluing down the shapes.

† Geometric shapes lend themselves to artistic endeavors. Using only triangles, try to fit the shapes into a design. You can do this with one color of pencil or with cut out shapes. A fun activity is to create a fish design. This lends itself well to the triangle shape, especially the fins.

† Create a picture using a computer-generated drawing program. Most computers have a file under accessories called "paint." Become familiar with this program. Computer-generated art is very difficult to create but fun once the tricks are learned.

† Design a puzzle from your computer-generated drawing (or another drawing you don't mind cutting up). Glue the picture to a poster board or other stiff paper. Carefully cut out the shapes using templates.

Music

† Make your own "Creation" music tapes. Write songs set to popular tunes, such as "Row, Row, Row your Boat." Change the words to fit what you have been studying in this unit, and teach them to a young child.

† Use different instruments to simulate nature sounds. What can you use for a bird, a wolf, or a bear? Do certain types of music remind you of animals? Listen to a classical music soundtrack such as "Peter and the Wolf." What does the music call to mind? Study classical music.

† Study classical composers. Many of them were Christian and composed music for church services. Do a study of this.

† Study the layout of an orchestra. Compare this to the orchestra when it began. How is the layout of the instruments different? What instruments are used in today's orchestra that

were not used years ago? Who conducted the orchestra in years past? How has this changed today?

† Study Beethoven's *Pastoral* Symphony. It is said to be less dramatic than some of his others, but it conveyed the passing scenes and moods of the countryside, describing sounds such as a flowing stream, birdcalls, thunder, and the sun coming out after a storm. No one before Beethoven had ever attempted to make music "paint" a picture. This was an example of a certain type of music. What was it? (Romantic, a term which described sentimental music as well as art and literature of the nineteenth century.)

† Talent is often considered by Christians to be a gift from God. This is due in part to the young age at which many famous composers created music. Research gifted young composers of today.

† If you have musical talent, try composing music. Sit outdoors and listen to the sounds of nature. Try to create tones or notes that may portray some of these sounds.

Creation Science Outline
9-12

Refer to Teaching Outline for more detailed information.

I. Days of Creation
    A. Twenty-four-hour time periods; Hebrew word *yom* means regular day
    B. Day One — Light and dark
    C. Day Two — Waters above and waters below
        1. Water vapor canopy
        2. Increased atmospheric pressure — benefits to longevity and increased size
        3. Shielded from harmful radiation — increased longevity
            (see timeline on page vi)
        4. Tropical environment worldwide and no storms
        5. Waters below — fountains of the great deep
    D. Day Three — Dry land and plants
    E. Day Four — Sun, moon, and stars
        1. Light before sun
        2. Stars for signs and to mark seasons, days, years
    F. Day Five — Birds and fish
    G. Day Six — All other animals and Man
II. Explain False Concepts
    A. Theistic evolution
    B. Day-age theory
    C. Gap theory
III. Flood Geology and Noah's Ark
    A. Ark designed by God — dimensions and capacity
    B. Gen. 7:11 — fountains of great deep burst forth, and it rained for the first time
    C. Most geological formations we see were formed during the Flood, others
        soon after.
    D. Water-lain sediments and aquatic fossils on every mountain top
    E. Earth's axis tilts
        1. Now we have seasons
        2. Formation of polar ice caps/ Ice Age
    F. Evidence for worldwide flood — interpretation fits physical evidence
        1. Fossil fish in swimming position — fossil insects with outspread wings
        2. Only preserved by rapid burial
        3. Submarine canyons cut by receding water — Guyots
        4. Mt. Saint Helens and the Grand Canyon
        5. Plate tectonics and continental sprint
IV. Evidence for Young Earth
    A. Radiometric age dating shown to be false — false assumptions
        1. A 170-year-old volcanic eruption misdated 160 million to 3 billion
            years
        2. Problems with carbon dating
    B. Alpha particles — Larry Vardiman

      C. Polonium halos — Robert Gentry

      D. Oil well fluid pressures — personal experience

      E. Erosion — not enough sediment in ocean basins — more rapid in past

      F. Stalactites forming in buildings — bat encased in stalactite

      G. Coral reef

      H. Niagara Falls

      I. Sea salinity and dissolved minerals

      J. Crustal buildup

      K. Sun is young

V. Big Bang Theory

      A. Red shift due to gravitational mass of object

      B. Cold dark matter

      C. Everything started from nothing and then exploded

      D. *Time* magazine article

VI. Energy and Entropy

      A. First Law of Thermodynamics

      B. Second Law of Thermodynamics

VII. Problems with Darwinian Theory

      A. No macroevolution

      B. Each new change must be beneficial

      C. Dog breeding — always get a dog (microevolution)

      D. Donkey and horse — mule that cannot reproduce

VIII. DNA, Proteins, Amino Acids, and Sugars

      A. Left & right-handed molecules — only left in living organisms

      B. Biological DNA and protein

      C. Possible combinations & random chance

      D. DNA is made using proteins (enzymes); protein is coded by DNA which is the blueprint; which came first?

IX. Ernst Haeckel — "Ontogeny recapitulates phylogeny" lie

      A. Gill slits — not respiration

      B. Yolk sac — not nourishment

      C. Tail bone — not tail

X. Human Senses

      A. Ear — complex structures

      B. Eye — works with brain to combine four sources of information

      C. Smell and taste — incredible combinations

      D. Touch — marvelous sensory range

XI. Fossil Record

      A. No evidence of any transitional fossils

      B. Stasis and extinction

      C. No jellyfish to vertebrate fish; no reptile to bird;

      D. No evolution — fossil creatures look identical to those of today

XII. Deliberate Hoaxes and Bad Science
    A. Neanderthal Man — new information questions findings
    B. Piltdown Man — altered ape jaw with teeth filed down and stained to look old
    C. Lucy — precise measurements made from crushed bones (very bad science)
    D. Java Man — ape skull with human leg
    E. Nebraska Man — pig's tooth, now out of textbooks

XIII. What Scientists Believe Is Always Changing
    A. Frogs from ponds
    B. Maggots from meat
    C. Flies and rats from garbage
    D. Mice from sweaty shirt and grain
    E. Spontaneous Generation proven false by Louis Pasteur — "Life always comes from life." — The Law of Biogenesis
    F. Earth center of universe

XIV. Other Facts
    A. Molecular biology — does not support evolution
    B. Temple of Amen-Ra — evidence of axial tilt and wobble
    C. Mount St. Helens — rapid deposition and erosion
    D. Neutron capture by Lead — not from Ur 238 decay
    E. Flow rate of basalt — if the moon were old, the craters would have smoothed out instead of maintaining sharp edges
    F. Galaxy clusters vs. field galaxies
    G. Polystrate fossils — evidence of rapid deposition

Lesson Plans

Week 1 — Creation
9-12

Subject	Monday	Tuesday	Wednesday	Thursday	Friday
Date:					
Bible/Religion Studies	Gen. 1:1-8	Gen. 1:9-19	Gen. 1:20-31	Gen. 2:1-25	TS
Creation Teaching Outline	I. A-B	I. C-D	I. E-G		
Reading Selection	Days 1-2 CR	Days 3-4 CR	Days 5-6 CR	Day 7 God rested	TS CR
Language Arts	Pre-test vocabulary words; assign ten	Develop an idea for a term paper on science topic; research	Use a paragraph from Genesis for dictation	Research the word "covenant" in the Bible	Write the Creation story in your own words
Math Reinforcement	Research the calendar system	Draw a graph of the abundance of life in Cambrian period	Write a conversion table for inches, feet, yards, miles into metric units	What is terminal velocity?	Study the mathematical formulas around us
Science Activities and Experiments **Creation Week**	How did the universe begin?	TS	Find the volumes of various shapes	Study the steps of the scientific method.; use and explain	Choose an experiment and complete using scientific method
Geography/History World Map or Globe	Review map skills and terminology	Map Identification: beginning of civilization	Timeline from Adam to Abraham	Research when scientists began to doubt Creation	Compare various forms of geography
Art/Music	Colored chalk art	Orderliness of music	Make a bread basket	Music off key activity	

CR= Creation Resource

TS= Teacher Selection

Lesson Plans

Subject Date:	Monday	Tuesday	Wednesday	Thursday	Friday
Bible/Religion Studies	Gen. 6: 9-22	TS	Gen. 8: 1-22	TS	Gen. 7: 17-24
Creation Teaching Outline	II. A-B	II. C.	III. A-B	III. C-D.	III. E-F
Reading Selection	False concepts	Gap theory	Ark design and fountains of the deep	Geologic form; sediments	Earth's axis; worldwide flood
Language Arts	Assign ten words from list	Write a report on the gap theory pro & con	Write sentences and label parts of speech	Write a "call to action" paper	Respond to news article with editorial
Math Reinforcement	Calculate the Ark's capacity	Ratio of a cubit to a foot	Mathematics of Ark dimensions	Equation of force	TS
Science Activities and Experiments False Concepts & Geology	Research types of beliefs in Creation	Sedimentary experiment	Sink or float—devise an experiment	Study the Grand Canyon	Laws of planetary motion
Geography/History World Map or Globe	History of Geology	TS	Locate Mt. Ararat. Research for information about early civilization found there	Read and study ancient geologists	Chart early civilizations that claim "flood" stories
Art/Music	Begin a nature journal; record observations and sketch or photograph findings	Press flowers	TS	Study music history	TS

CR= Creation Resource

TS= Teacher Selection

Lesson Plans

Week 3 — Evidence for Young Earth
9-12

Subject Date:	Monday	Tuesday	Wednesday	Thursday	Friday
Bible/Religion Studies	Exodus 20:11 Exodus 20:1-17	Psalm 102:25	Psalm 104	Psalm 119:30	TS
Creation Teaching Outline	IV. A	IV. B-D	IV. E-G	IV. H-J	IV. K
Reading Selection	Radiometric dating	Alpha particles; Polonium halos; oil well	Erosion; stalactites; coral reefs	Niagara Falls; sea salinity; crustal buildup	Young sun
Language Arts	Assign ten words from list	Write paper on topic from this week's outline	Write a paragraph on erosion in your area or state	Research Niagara Falls and rate of erosion	Play vocabulary game
Math Reinforcement	Assumptions of ^{14}C dating	Percentages of fossils finds	Study growth rates of stalactites from Creationist perspective	Rates of coral reef growth, sea salt and crustal buildup	TS
Science Activities and Experiments Evidence for a Young Earth	Energy and burning wood	Explain uniformitarianism	Study soil structure and devise experiment; use a store bought kit to determine properties	Read abstracts from ICR or AIG website about young earth	Demonstrate air pressure; crush a can activity
Geography/History World Map or Globe	Study Blaise Pascal		Study Charles Lyell		Study recent Creation scientists
Art/Music	Create sand art	Study various musical instruments show orderliness	Cut out various magazine pictures and make a montage	Continue nature journal	Create an original tune or song

CR= Creation Resource

TS= Teacher Selection

Lesson Plans

Subject Date:	Monday	Tuesday	Wednesday	Thursday	Friday
Bible/Religion Studies	Psalm 147: 4-5	TS	Psalm 148	TS	Psalm 146:5-6
Creation Teaching Outline	V.	VI. A-B	VII. A-C	VIII. A-B	VIII. C-D
Reading Selection	Big Bang	Energy and entropy	Darwinian concepts	DNA and protein	Random chance; enzymes
Language Arts	Assign remainder of vocabulary	Write a brief overview of fossil record	Reporter: write a piece on uncovering frauds of evolution	Write a poetic piece about topic of choice	Play vocabulary game or create a puzzle
Math Reinforcement	Research statistics of big bang actually happening	What is a parabolic curve?	Explain acceleration of falling body	Probability coin flips	Explain random chance
Science Activities and Experiments Big Bang; Thermodynamics	Big Bang experiment	Entropy activity	Thermodynamics experiment Hot coffee	Proteins are called the building blocks of cells, research	Plan a menu and analyze the nutritional content
Geography/History World Map or Globe	What was happening during the time that Darwin lived?	Study a geological map online	Research scientists that studied the properties of light	Look for DNA models online	Study Kepler
Art/Music	Create sculpture using materials found in nature	Make musical instruments	Work on nature journal	Study well-known Christian artists	

CR= Creation Resource

TS= Teacher Selection

Lesson Plans

Subject Date:	Monday	Tuesday	Wednesday	Thursday	Friday
Bible/Religion Studies	Psalm 33:6-11	Psalm 34:8	Psalm 34:11-20	TS	TS
Creation Teaching Outline	IX. A-C	X. A-D	XI. A-C	XI. D-E	XII. A-E
Reading Selection	Haeckel	Human senses	Fossil record	No evolution proof	Hoaxes and bad science
Language Arts	Assign remaining words from list	Play vocabulary card game	Write short story on evolutionary hoaxes	Mock debate with evolutionist	Key spokesperson for ICR
Math Reinforcement	Geometric shapes show orderliness		Mathematical data dating fossil record	Statistics of evolution	
Science Activities and Experiments Concepts, Senses, and Fossil Record	Research Haeckel	Dust collectors	Research conditions needed for fossils to form	Explain abrupt fossil record	Devise experiment using senses
Geography/History World Map or Globe		Map geographic areas where dinosaurs have been excavated	Map of Australia	Map and locate ancient structures that defy explanation such as Stonehenge	
Art/Music	Create cave art	Create musical instrument	Braid rope	Use geometric shapes to create proportional art	Study ancient musical instruments

CR= Creation Resource   TS= Teacher Selection

Lesson Plans

Subject Date:	Monday	Tuesday	Wednesday	Thursday	Friday
Bible/Religion Studies	Psalm 37:1-13	Psalm 40:1-5	Psalm 42	Psalm 89:5-17	Job 38
Creation Teaching Outline	XIII. A-B	XIII. D-F	XIV. A-B	XIV. C-D	XIV. E-G
Reading Selection	Frogs, maggots, and flies	Mice; spontaneous generation; earth as center of univ.	Molecular biology; Temple of Amen-Ra	Mt. St. Helens; neutron capture	Basalt; galaxy clusters; polystrate fossils
Language Arts	Review vocabulary words; play game	Crossword puzzle or word search	Term paper on one theme from outline ——————————————→		
Math Reinforcement		Ancient man		Fibonacci	
Science Activities and Experiments Light & Dark ; Water	Law of Biogenesis	Redi experiment	Observe a leaf or insect with a compound microscope draw findings	Geologic column	Properties of matter
Geography/History World Map or Globe	Locate sites of recent archaeological and paleontological discoveries	Study scientific discoveries of Pasteur	What events of historical significance remain unexplained? Research	Locate Mt. St. Helens and research before and after volcanic eruption	
Art/Music		Picture a tune; look at a musical bar and draw a graph		Complete nature journal	

LA= Language Arts   CR= Creation Resource   TS= Teacher Selection

Reading List
9-12

The Answers Book by Ken Ham, Andrew Snelling, and Carl Wieland (Master Books, 2000, 207 pages). This book provides answers to twelve of the most frequently asked questions on the subject of Creation.

Darwin on Trial by Phillip E. Johnson (InterVarsity Press, 1991, 195 pages). This is written by a lawyer who uses logic and reason to submit the scientific support for Darwinism to careful scrutiny. He finds that the theory of evolution is severely lacking in confirmatory evidence.

Dinosaurs, The Lost World, & You by John D. Morris, Ph.D. (Master Books, 1999, 48 pages). A very good book explaining where the dinosaurs fit into the Creation account in the book of Genesis. This also deals with the vast amount of misinformation the media portrays relating to dinosaurs.

Evolution: The Fossils Still Say No by Dr. Duane T. Gish (Institute of Creation Research, 1995, 391 pages). A critical evaluation of the fossil record using documents from the evolutionists themselves. This points to the total absence of any transitional forms.

Evolution: Theory in Crisis by Michael Denton (Adler and Adler, 1986, 365 pages). This is a book written by a non-Creationist biochemist who gives an accurate account of the evolutionary crisis. He explains in a factual and objective examination of the evidence that the simple elements of life are really not very simple at all.

The Genesis Solution by Ken Ham and Paul Taylor (Master Books, 1997, 126 pages). A great book on the fundamental accuracy of Genesis and its importance to the Christian faith.

Grand Canyon: Monument to Catastrophe by Dr. Steve Austin (Institute of Creation Research, 1994, 284 pages). It explains how the Grand Canyon could have formed as one of the aftereffects of Noah's flood. It compares the formation of the Grand Canyon to the formations after the eruption at Mt. St. Helens.

The Lie: Evolution by Ken Ham (Master Books, 1987, 168 pages). Arms Christians with the information to defend their faith, the Gospel message, Genesis, and Creation. Full of humorous drawings and Ken Ham's wit.

Origins: Creation or Evolution by Richard Bliss (Master Books, 1988, 76 pages). A basic and concise summary of Creation Science. Fully illustrated.

Origin of Life by Richard Bliss, Gary Parker, and Duane Gish (Creation Life Publishers, 1979, 51 pages). This book deals with the questions of when, where, and how life began.

The Puzzle of Ancient Man (Advanced Technology in Past Civilizations?) by Donald E. Chittick (Creation Compass, 1998, 182 pages). One of my favorite books and a must-read for anyone interested in the intelligence of our ancestors. A fantastic example of information confounding scientists of today.

Streams of Civilization, Volume One by Mary Stanton and Albert Hyma (Creation-Life Publishers, 1992, 410 pages). A good resource that provides a complete overview of history from Creation to the discovery of America. Great book!

Unlocking the Mysteries of Creation by Dennis Petersen (Creation Research Foundation, 1986, 205 pages). This book is an excellent first book on Creation science. The many topics discussed will inspire you to dig further into the study of Creation science.

The Young Earth by Dr. John Morris (Master Books, 1994, 288 pages). This book explains how true science supports a young earth and problems of major dating methods. Simple explanation of scientific terms.

	amino acids		instantaneous
	speed of light		radiometric dating
	half-life		probability
	polonium halos		geomorphology
	ecological zones		chronometer
	entropy		relativity
	thermodynamics		extrapolating
	cosmology		weathering
	pores		porosity
	reservoir rock		geosyncline
	stratigraphy		taxonomy
	stratigrapher		uniformitarianism
	paleontologist		seismic waves
	palynologist		magnetic field
	hydrologist		alpha particles
	diastrophism		discontinuity
	hyperbaric		unconformity
	seismologist		subduction zone
	hydrostatic pressure		epicenter
	oceanography		fractals
	geophysics		vectors
	index fossil		Mohorovicic discontinuity
	deoxyribonucleic acid		parabolic

Vocabulary/Spelling/Grammar Ideas
9-12

✝ Use the vocabulary and spelling words interchangeably in the following activities.

✝ Give a pre-test of spelling and vocabulary words. This is a good indication of the words that need to be studied. Dictate the words or put them on audiocassette. Students can spell them and give a brief definition of each word.

✝ Look up the words in a dictionary, science dictionary, encyclopedia, or online. Write brief definitions for each word. Write the words into sentences using a variety of the parts of speech. Place the definitions on index cards to use in other activities or make up your own game.

✝ Use the sentences to label (or diagram) parts of speech. Use resources such as a good grammar handbook to check your answers.

✝ Use the vocabulary words to write a paragraph or story. Check for proper spelling, punctuation, usage, and form. Use a variety of sentence openers. Most people begin with subject and verb as openings for sentences. Try varying this approach using a preposition; words that end in "ly" or "ing"; clausal words such as although, since, while, where, as, if, etc.; very short sentences; and words that end in "ed."

✝ Make a list of words that you cannot use in writing your sentences, such as said, like, go, nice, pretty, see. Start a taboo word list and add to this list of overused words. Make an attempt to broaden your vocabulary with words that stretch the imagination. Use a thesaurus or invest in a handheld spell checker or computer-generated dictionary. Use these resources and watch your writing improve dramatically.

✝ Have the student make a crossword puzzle using the vocabulary words. Try to use the definitions you have researched. (Let the parents try, too!)

✝ Have students create a word search puzzle on a large poster board. Put in as many of the vocabulary words as possible.

✝ Try finding as many smaller words within the vocabulary words as possible. List these. Which word contains the most small words?

✝ Keep a list of words you may not know the meaning of from your reading. Look up these words and keep a vocabulary list. Try to use these new words daily if the opportunity arises.

✝ Define the words archaeologist, anthropologist, and paleontologist. Compare and contrast these scientists. What type of education is necessary to become one of these individuals?

† Use the vocabulary words to create a game. Place the more difficult words on cards such as polonium halos, thermodynamics, subduction zone, etc. Then place the true definition on the back of the card. Shuffle and place the cards face down. One player, the scorekeeper, draws a card (he is the only one who knows the true definition of the word). He says the word, "thermodynamics" for example. Each person must write his own definition of the word on slips of paper. They can be silly, far fetched, or accurate. The definitions are collected by the scorekeeper. He reads the word again and the collected definitions as well as the real definition. If someone has stated the real definition, he can choose to omit repeating it twice. Everyone votes on what they believe the true definition is. The person who created the winning definition gets the "tally" of votes, whether the definition is correct or not. This is a way to become familiar with the words in an entertaining manner. The next person in line takes a turn becoming the scorekeeper until everyone has had a turn. The game may be played as long as you wish or until all the definitions have been read.

Language Arts
9-12

† God is the Great Creator of the Heavens. He has assigned each of the stars a specific place. Read Psalm 19:1-4 as a Christian astronomer and write what it means in your own words.

† The Bible is a great science book. Read Psalm 104. Make a list of the scientific observations in this chapter.

† Read the Book of Job. What does God say about Creation? Make a list of all references to Creation.

† Read *The Origin of Species* by Charles Darwin. Be aware of this chapter (Chapter 6) admitting difficulties with his own theory of evolution. Compare it to the Biblical account of specific Creation (Genesis 1-2) in about 250 words.

† Write down the pros and cons of Creation vs. evolution under each heading, Creation Pro and Con, Evolution Pro and Con. Try for six or seven of each.

† Explain the difficulty of a transitional creature trying to function while it is evolving. Write a fictional account of a creature with five percent of a new eye or five percent of a new wing. What difficulties would he encounter? Would there be any benefits? How would it find food, shelter, a mate, grow and reproduce? Draw pictures to accompany your story.

† Where is the evidence of transitional fossils? Write a brief overview (100 words) of what the fossil record actually shows. Your explanation should include the words "stasis" and "extinction" in the proper context.

† Pretend you are a reporter and write an article for a newspaper called the *Creation Times*. Write a exposé in 250 words or less uncovering fraud in evolutionary claims. (Hint: Piltdown Man.)

† Does the Bible teach that the Earth is flat? What Scripture did Columbus use to indicate (for himself) that the Earth was a sphere? When did people first calculate the circumference of the earth?

† You are the key spokesperson for the Creation Institute in your hometown. A newspaper reporter has left a message on your cell phone informing you that the "Missing Link" has been found. He wants to hear your response to this extraordinary find. What research will you do before calling him back? What facts will you gather to counteract his claims? Write a 200-word rebuttal.

† Many people now claim they do believe in evolution, but not neo-Darwinian evolution.

What do they mean by this? What is their explanation for how the world began?

† What is Intelligent Design, and how does this differ from Creationists' claims? In what ways are they similar?

† Many secular scientists of today think that evolution is the only thing they can believe in because the alternative is unbearable for them. Explain what this does to their scientific analysis when studying the fossil record. How does an ingrained bias affect your observation? Explain how a Creationist and an evolutionist can look at the same information, such the Grand Canyon, and yet see two completely different things.

† Write an article for a publication as a "call to action" that will be a wake-up call for Christians to be more verbal in regard to the Creation/evolution debate. Give them plenty of evidence to use in their encounter with non-believers.

† The Bible tells us to have a ready answer when asked why we believe the way we do. Write out your answer in about 200 words. Include some Creation science evidence.

† Research fossil fish. Examine as many photographs as are available in your library. Notice how well preserved the details are. There are photos of preserved fossil fish giving birth, eating another fish, etc. Explain that this type of preservation requires rapid burial.

† Write an argument against the earliest people being unintelligent, slow, and not very clever. Use the Bible verses that talk about all the skills Adam's descendants had. Everyone on the planet ultimately came from Noah and his family. The first descendants of those eight would have had all the accumulated wisdom and experience of this man of great age.

† Scientists have discovered cave drawings (twenty-five of them so far) in Australia that have been deciphered to be maps of constellations. Some cave drawings are believed to be maps of the lunar cycle (*Creation*, 1994). Explain how this is a problem for evolutionists' perceptions of "primitive man."

† Make a list of all the supplies needed to build and furnish the Ark. You will need to calculate the wood needed for its size, the number of levels, the number of cages, water and feed troughs, and food for the animals and people.

† Look up archaeological discoveries of the so-called "Stone Age." Is there any evidence to suggest that these people were actually skilled workers and not simply primitive? How do evolutionists explain bowls, plates, and artfully decorated vases that have been uncovered?

† Peruse your local newspaper daily for several weeks. Notice any articles or editorials that have an evolutionary bias and write down the terminology used. Also be aware of the anti-

Creationist bias and write down those terms. Learn to always recognize and be aware of opinion and bias in whatever you read.

† Read and write a summary of a biography of Wernher von Braun. Von Braun was instrumental in the pioneering work on rockets for space exploration. Who was his inspiration at age thirteen? Who was the first man to set foot on the moon?

† Read through the New Testament, making note of the times Jesus quotes from the Old Testament. Keep track of the Scriptures and list them by book.

† Study the benefits of an organic food diet. Why do grocery-store foods lack taste? What has happened to the nutritional value of today's food as compared to one hundred years ago? Write an analysis of your findings. Try growing your own tomatoes or strawberries.

† In your own words, explain the point of this Scripture: Romans 1:20, "For since the creation of the world God's invisible qualities—his eternal power and divine nature—have been clearly seen, being understood from what has been made, so that men are without excuse."

† The Bible refers to Jesus as light (John 8:12). Write a comparison of the properties of natural light and Jesus the Light of the World. How does an understanding of the properties of light help you to understand Jesus?

† Watch a Creation science video (see the resource section on page 138 for a good selection) and write a movie review. Enjoy it with some popcorn!

† You are a reporter for Channel 7 News and you have been assigned to cover the story of some guy building a large wooden structure on the side of a mountain. There is a big ruckus going on around the construction site with people partying and making fun of the construction crew. After several days of your investigation you file your report for your boss. This man has no permits; OSHA (Occupational Safety and Health Administration) wanted him to install a sprinkler system; the EPA (Environmental Protection Agency) is getting on his case for cutting down too many trees; etc. Write out your report.

† The Bible states that wisdom is something we should seek after. Search through the Proverbs and make a list of all the Scriptures that talk about wisdom.

† Read the biography of Leonardo Fibonacci, the man who discovered the mathematical beauty in nature. What are the Fibonacci numbers?

† For an interesting study in human nature, see how many people you can get to sign a petition that demands the elimination of dihydrogen monoxide (good old H_2O). Write out a complaint against dihydrogen monoxide since: (1) it is the major component in acid rain, (2)

it can cause severe burns in its gaseous state, (3) accidental inhalation can kill you, (4) it contributes to erosion, (5) it decreases the effectiveness of automobile brakes, and (6) it has been found in tumors of patients with terminal cancer. Summarize your results.

† Research Greek mythology surrounding Nereus and compare the account of this figure to Noah and the Flood. Find pictures of Nereus in Greek art.

† Psalm 19:2 says, "The heavens declare the glory of God." Write a page on what that means to you. Back up your thoughts with scripture and creation science information.

† Start a collection of stamps that show God's beautiful Creation. Collect stamps of animals, plants, stars, mountains, or whatever is of interest to you.

† Look at the penguins of the Antarctic. These amazing creatures are perfectly designed for life in the extreme climate of the South Pole. How could birds have evolved the special features necessary for penguins to live there? Write a rebuttal to the evolutionists' claim that these birds evolved to live there.

† Plan a research paper. Decide on a topic and how you will develop your thesis sentence. Research the topic thoroughly on websites such as www.icr.org or www.creationresearch.org. Make sure your information is well documented, using the standard forms for documentation. Research how to do a research paper! This is very good preparation for college or other higher education.

Mathematics and Probability
9-12

✝ How does random chance work? Roll a die six times and try to get one through six in sequential order. (Repeat this process several times.) What is the probability of obtaining this outcome? Chart your results.

✝ Record the results of twenty-five coins "flipped" at one time. What is the probability that you will get twenty-five heads at one time? Repeat this process several times and record the outcomes. Relate this to the formation of DNA chains, which have to contain one hundred percent left-handed molecules in order to be useful to living organisms.

✝ What assumptions are used in radiometric dating? What are some faults with these assumptions? (See Teaching Outline section IV.)

✝ Calculate the capacity (volume) of the Ark (Gen. 6:15) in feet, cubits, and meters.

✝ What is the ratio of a cubit to a foot?

✝ How long did it take to build the Ark? How long were Noah and his family in the Ark?

✝ What is a parabolic curve?

✝ What measuring system is used in scientific experiments? Why?

✝ Write a conversion table. Convert inches, feet, yards, and miles into metric units. For fun, convert cubits into metric units.

✝ The Law of Gravity states: the force of gravity is proportional to the product of the two masses and inversely proportional to the square of the distance between their centers of mass. [Gravitational force = $(G \times m_1 \times m_2)/d^2$] What is the equation for Force? [$F=ma$] What is the formula for the earth's gravitational force? [weight = mass x gravity; gravity = weight divided by mass; gravity equals the force of attraction between two masses: $F=Gm_1m_2/r^2$.] What is Newton's gravitational constant? [$9.8m/s^2$, where m=mass and s=seconds; this is the same thing as gravitation at the earth's surface.] Explain acceleration of a falling body. [32 feet per second per second] This may be oral or written.

✝ What is terminal velocity? Why does a falling body reach a terminal velocity? (Wind resistance.)

✝ In Biblical times man lived much longer than he does today. List some of the ages of ancient man from Biblical records. How was the age of the earth determined? Research this.

† Study sea-floor sedimentary layers. Read an abstract on this topic from a Creation resource or a Creation website such as www.icr.org or www.creationresearch.org. What does the rate of sedimentation show? How is this calculated?

† Has the rate of stalactite and stalagmite growth been charted using non-evolutionary sources? Research this and calculate the growth of the stalactites under the Lincoln Monument in Washington, D.C.

† Research the erosion rate of Niagara Falls. The point of origin is known. What does this tell us? Calculate how many years it would take for Niagara Falls to completely erode at the rate of erosion today.

† What are some common assumptions about [14]carbon dating? What is the statistical evidence pointing to the error rate of this method of age dating? Are there other forms of age dating that are more accurate? Research this.

† Study erosion factors. What mathematical basis is used to determine these rates? What is taken into consideration when determining whether a coral reef, for example, has grown or if there has been erosion to our shorelines.

† What would be the statistical probability of the Big Bang really happening? Devise a mathematical problem determining this.

† What mathematical data exists which determines percentages of fossils that have been found in the world? If the world were billions of years old, there should be fossilized remains of man all over the world. This isn't happening. What are the statistics of fossilization of invertebrate, vertebrate, etc?

The following activities are variations taken from the book *Math Wizardry for Kids*:(Barrons, 1995). This book is highly recommended.

† Discovering mathematics in nature is as old as the beginning of time. There are mathematical formulas all around us. Ancient Greeks called patterns of proportion the golden mean or golden proportion. They regarded these patterns as precious as gold because they contained beauty and balance . The Greeks named this proportion for Phidias, an ancient Greek sculptor, and shortened the name to Φ or phi. The exact formula is $(1 + \sqrt{5})/2$. Use a calculator to figure out the answer. (1.6) Do a word search online for Phidias.

† Using the above proportion apply it to everyday life. If a small section of artwork, for example, is 1 part, the large section should be 1.6. If the large section is 1 part, then the small section should be .06. When things are asthetically pleasing, it is normally due to the proportion of the work. Try to make these observations in nature.

† Relate the Fibonacci numbers to the golden proportion. (For information on Fibonacci numbers use the library or do a key word search online.) Find the first ten Fibonacci numbers (see the 4-8 mathematics section on page 88). Now, using your calculator, divide each Fibonacci number by the next higher number in the series. One way to state the golden proportion is that if the long side of the shape is 1, the short side is 0.618034. How long does is take before the numbers you divide come close to 0.618034? Now do the reverse. Use your calculator to divide each Fibonacci number by the next lower number in the series. The other way of stating the golden proportion is if the short side of a shape is 1, then the long side is 1.618034. How long does it take before the numbers you divide come close to 1.618034? (The higher you go with the Fibonacci numbers, the closer you get to the golden mean. The two concepts show the same proportions of nature's math and point to the orderliness of God's awesome creation!)

† Archeologists have uncovered information about past civilizations and have had to learn to decipher "dead" languages. Research this phenomenon. For example, Napoleon accidentally found the Rosetta Stone while his troops were digging trenches in Egypt. This stone tablet contained information about the Egyptian language that had never been completely deciphered until that time. Devise a code of your own to be deciphered. Give each letter of the alphabet a symbol or number. Devise a secret message and ask someone to decode it.

† What are the mathematics of music? Research this and the importance of math in understanding music as well as science!

† Many of us could not imagine life without a calculator. Yet they were nonexistent in the times of Noah and his clan. The abacus was used in ancient times as a method of adding difficult numbers. Research the abacus and learn when it was replaced and by what type of instrument? When did modern devices first begin to be used?

† Binary codes are used by computers. The binary code consists of only 1's and 0's. Research this method of calculation and study artificial intelligence.

Science Activities and Experiments
9-12

† According to the Big Bang theory, how did the universe begin? Create your own "Big Bang" with a paper bag. Fill a paper bag with twenty Popsicle sticks. Inflate the bag and pop it. Do the Popsicle sticks form a house (or any distinct pattern or design)? How can you get order from chaos?

† What is the basis for Darwinian evolution? What is uniformitarianism? List some of the problems with a uniformitarian approach.

† What was the world like prior to the Flood? Describe what you think the "pre-Flood earth" (antediluvian) looked like. Use the Bible for ideas. Describe the post-Flood earth and make a comparison.

† Find at least three scientific ideas that were stated in the Bible long before science discovered them. For example: Isaiah 40:22 says, "He sits enthroned above the circle of the earth" (Isaiah was written around 760 B.C.) Job 38:7 says that at creation the stars sang, but radio-astronomers did not hear it until the 1950s.

† What does "science" mean? Does the Bible have to fit into science? Should science fit into the Bible? Is the Creation process or the evolution process repeatable in a laboratory? If it is not science, what is it? Write a one-page paper explaining your thoughts.

† What is the Law of Biogenesis, and who stated it? Boil chicken broth, put it into a jar with a tight-fitting lid, and observe for several weeks. Is anything growing from this broth? What do you see? Record your results. (Francesco Redi's original experiment, still on display in a museum in France, shows no growth.)

† What did Francesco Redi prove? Try his experiment. With your mother's approval, put raw meat scraps in each of three jars. Leave one open, cover one with gauze held by a rubber band, and seal one tightly with a lid. Leave jars outside on a porch if possible (or in a house where many flies are present!). Observe for several days, and record your observations. What happened in each jar? How does this show that spontaneous generation does not occur?

† What is wrong with the fossil record from Darwin's viewpoint? Are there any transitional forms of animals, plants, or people? If scientists found many transitional fossils, how would that affect the standard classification system?

† How does evolution explain the abrupt appearance of an abundance of life in the Cambrian period supposedly over 500 million years ago? Draw a graph of life found in the pre-Cambrian period vs. life found in the Cambrian period. Nearly every phylum is found in the Cambrian, including completely vertebrate fish. How does the specific creation of "kinds"

better explain this abrupt occurrence?

† What does evolution need to achieve complexity besides a mechanism for change? (Time) If you have to assemble a bicycle, can you do it better in two days, two weeks, or two years? Does the addition of more time help improve the chance of proper assembly? Why is intelligence necessary to achieve assembly? If you have enough intelligence, do you need a long period of time to accomplish anything?

† Briefly define thermodynamics in general and explain its laws. (See Teaching Outline section VI.)

† Explain entropy. Perform an example of entropy and explain how this does or does not support evolution. Mix a solution of 3 parts sand and 1 part plaster of Paris with enough water to make a thick mixture, and pour into a mold (an old butter tub, etc.) After setting, unmold and place outdoors. Observe and record what happens to the plaster for several weeks. This is best done during the warm, rainy season. Does the plaster of Paris begin to deteriorate or become more complex? What happens? Record your observations. Does this support the Second Law of Thermodynamics?

† What did Aristotle's model of the universe look like? Draw a diagram to represent an earth-centered system rather than a solar system.

† How was Copernicus's model of the universe different from Aristotle's? Draw a diagram to represent this solar system. What does our solar system look like? What is the difference?

† Who discovered the three laws of planetary motion? What are these three laws? How would you create an experiment to test each of these laws? Use the scientific method.

† How are energy and matter related? Observe a piece of wood burning. (The matter contained in the wood is translated into heat and light energy that can be felt and observed.)

† Explain the universal law of gravitation. How did Kepler's discovery help Newton establish the law of gravity? Demonstrate the "gravitational attraction" of two planetary bodies. Place a bowling ball on a trampoline (or a water bed or soft cushion). Notice how the surface is distorted. Place a small ball on the edge of the trampoline (or other surface). What happens? Find the formula for the gravitational attraction between two planetary bodies. How does distance affect attraction?

† Lead the following discussion and activities explaining Thermodynamics to your children:
Place a cup of hot coffee (or other hot liquid) on the table.
Question: Will this coffee stay hot? (Answer: No.)
Question: Why not? (Answer: It cools off.)

Question: Why does it cool off? (Answer: The heat dissipates, disperses, spreads out, etc.)

Question: Does the energy from the heat disappear? (Answer: No.)

Explain: Energy has a tendency to even out in the air and all over the universe. This is known as Entropy, or the Second Law of Thermodynamics. At the end of the activity (or perhaps some time later) measure the temperature of the coffee. Ask the children what happened to the heat. They should be able to tell you that heat is not lost; it has dispersed into the room.

(Variation: Wait to measure the temperature of the coffee until after the next activity.)

Drop a tennis ball from your hand held high. Have the children notice how each bounce rises shorter than the previous bounce until the ball rolls on the ground and stops. (Repeat this several times.)

Question: Will the ball return to my hand? (Answer: No.)

Question: Why not? (Answer: Because some of the energy is changed to heat as the ball pushes the air aside, and when the ball hits the ground both the ground and ball heat up slightly. Energy does not disappear; it changes to heat and spreads out in the air.)

Question: Where did the energy come from for bouncing? (Answer: You provided the potential energy to the ball when you lifted it. That took biochemical energy from your muscles that you get from eating food.)

Explain: Energy never comes out of nothing. Energy can never be created or destroyed, it can only be changed from one form or another. This is the Law of Conservation of Energy or the First Law of Thermodynamics.

Question: Where did I get the energy to move my arm to raise the ball? (Answer: The sun radiates energy as heat and light. Plants, such as vegetables and grass, store the energy. A cow eats the grass and the energy is used to move the cow around and some is stored. Then I eat a hamburger with lettuce and tomatoes, and the energy stored in the plants and the cow is changed into chemical energy in me. I use it to lift the ball [kinetic energy].) I give the ball potential energy until it drops. While dropping it has kinetic energy. The energy keeps changing.

† The geologic column can only be found in few places in the world. The Grand Canyon is a wonderful example of how the geologic column does not normally appear in a textbook sequence. Study this and explain the layering of the Grand Canyon and why it puzzles evolutionary scientists who do not believe the Flood was responsible for this awesome canyon.

† What conditions must take place for bones or other artifacts to remain preserved in the ground and become fossils? What would happen to items that were not covered by ideal conditions? Explain why rapid burial is required.

† What is one possible scientific explanation for the lack of an abundance of fossilized human remains if the earth is said to be millions or billions of years old? Fossil facts: Of all the fossils found to date, 95% are shallow water invertebrates (such as shellfish), 4.75% are algae and plants, 0.238% are insects and invertebrates, 0.0138 are fish, amphibian, reptile,

bird, and mammal, and 0.00125% are human bones.

† Draw and label the parts of an atom: nucleus, proton, neutron, electron. Make a three-dimensional model of an atom.

† List the nine steps of the Scientific Method and explain why it is important in working effectively. [Choose a problem; state what you think is the solution to the problem (your hypothesis); research what other scientists have done with similar problems; devise an experiment to prove or disprove your hypothesis; state your hypothesis as a theory if it is correct; state a new hypothesis if yours is incorrect and start over; after you have proved your hypothesis, write a paper on what you did to prove it; if new facts are discovered, change your theory; if the theory holds true after many years of testing, you may state it as a law.]

† What is scientific notation, and how can it be helpful when working with very large or very small numbers? Write out several very large and several very small numbers with many decimal places before them, and then express them in scientific notation.

† What is technology [applied science] and does it make science useful? List some technological devices that you use daily. What is the pure science behind them? List some ancient technology. [Hint: the wheel.]

† List the properties of matter and discuss. [volume: takes up space; weight: pull of the earth's gravity on an object; mass: the amount of matter in an object; density: the mass of a substance per unit of volume; buoyancy; freezing and boiling points; etc.] Pick several items and make a chart of their physical properties.

† Find the volume of various shaped objects. Pick small objects such as a rock, toy, ball, eraser, etc. Estimate their volume before measuring. Fill a graduated cylinder with water to one of the measuring lines and record the volume. Tie a string around each of the objects and lower them, one at a time, into the water. Now measure and record the level of the water. This is the volume of the water plus the object. Now subtract the original volume from your new volume; the difference is the volume of the object. Record all volumes on a chart and compare to your estimations. How close were you?

† Density is the mass of an object per unit of volume. Density is usually expressed in grams per cubic centimeter (g/cm^3). One cubic centimeter (volume) of water weighs 1 gram; therefore the density of water is 1 ($1gram/1cm^3$). Look up the density of various types of matter. Make a chart of densities as compared to water, with several less dense and several more dense.

† The air we breathe is full of microscopic particles, which you can see in a beam of sunlight. Make several dust collectors by cutting out a square of cardboard or particle board. Cut out

the middle of the board and fill it with tape or sheets of sticky paper used for removing lint from clothing. Place them in several places around your house where you think they will collect dust (record the locations) and leave them for about three days. Take them down, and observe and record what you have collected. Discuss how to filter the air we breathe.

† Create another demonstration of the crushing power of air on a tin can. You will need a one gallon, straight-sided can with a screw-on cap. (You can buy a new, empty kerosene or gasoline can at a hardware store.) Pour ½ cup of water into the can, place it on a burner, and bring to a boil for a few minutes. Remove the can from the stove into the sink, and when the amount of steam lessens somewhat, screw on the cap tightly. (You may want to have a parent do this.) Pour cold water over the can, and observe. [When first opened, the air inside the can equalized the air outside the can. When the water boiled, the steam replaced the air. The cold water caused the steam to condense into water and leave a vacuum in the can. With nothing inside to equalize the air pressure, the outside air crushed the can.]

† Construct a sundial. Search online for "Sundial Experiments" and pick one that suits you.

† Test your reaction time. Make a paper ruler 8 inches long with inches marked on it. Color it if you want to. Have another student hold the ruler by the top, and you stand with your hand ready to pinch it with your thumb and forefinger about an inch below the ruler. Have the first student drop the ruler, and you catch it. The closer to the bottom of the strip, the quicker your reaction time. Test the reaction times of several students. Record and plot a graph of all the times using the inch marks instead of a time value.

† Your heart has to pump against gravity. Stand in one place with one hand held as high as possible and the other hand allowed to hang down by your side. Hold this position for at least one minute (two is better). Now bring your hands together with palms up. What do you see? The hand that was held high is paler because gravity pulled some of the blood out of the hand. The hand that was held lower is darker because gravity caused the blood to pool there.

† Investigate some ancient structures such as Stonehenge, the faces of Easter Island, the Nasca Lines, the pyramids, etc. Get the facts on the weight of the stones or the length of the lines. What technology did these people use to make such massive structures? Would it be possible to move those heavy stones today? Speculate as to why they were constructed. Why were the Nasca lines drawn in a flat desert when they can only be seen from a high altitude?

† Order several prepared animals for dissection from one of the science resources listed in the back of the book.. Dissect and keep a photographic record of the process. Make note of any anomalies such as a worm in a frog's stomach.

† Research all you can about the amazing woodpecker. Write a one-page report about all the

special design elements of the woodpecker. Include at least the skull structure, the cushioning, the tongue, the legs, and the tailfeathers. Describe what would happen to an ordinary bird that tried to find food like a woodpecker. If woodpeckers live in your area, plan a bird-watching trip to look for them.

† Genesis 1 says that God created the lights in the sky (the entire universe) to give light to the Earth, for signs, and to mark the seasons, days, and years. Peter van de Kamp was a scientist who devoted his life to looking for other stars with planets. He claimed to have found them by observing the wobble of stars. Study his research and explain how his conclusion of wobbling stars was explained by the wobble of his telescope.

† Study a variety of insects such as a fly, bee, praying mantis, damselfly, ladybug, butterfly, moth, etc. Record the similarities and differences. List all the elements you find of special design and special function. Could these things have evolved by chance? Study these insects with a magnifying glass or compound microscope. What do you see? Draw results.

† Study the four different blood types; A, B, AB, and O. Which alleles, or gene variations, are dominant or recessive? How many possible combinations are there? If you do not know your own blood type, obtain a testing kit and find out.

† Research DNA models online. There are some wonderful websites that deal with the intricacies of DNA.

† Try your hand at reading scientific abstracts. Abstracts are the results of a scientist's experimentation or theory that has been developed by some type of in-depth research. Go to www.icr.org, www.answersingenesis.org, or www.creationresearch.org. Look up a specific topic that has been studied in this unit or one that has been presented and research additional information.

† Plan a nutritious meal and analyze the nutrient content. Try to use fresh or frozen foods rather than canned or pre-packaged.

† Some of the foods we purchase certainly were not what God intended when he created food to sustain our bodies. Try to read the labels of foods in the grocery store. Compare, for example, canned peaches to fresh or frozen. Compare the nutritional content of pasteurized milk with organic milk. What is the difference?

† Study soil structure and devise an experiment. Test various types of soil, such as rich compost and plain sandbox sand. Use a store-bought kit to determine the properties, or make your own determination by trying to grow potted plants in the various types of soil.

Geography/History Ideas
9-12

† On a world map look up the locations of archaeological, anthropological, and paleontological finds (dinosaurs, ancient cities, the Rosetta Stone, etc.).

† Study plate tectonics. What are the effects of continental sprint and drift? Where were the continents at one time? What is the term used to describe all the continents that were together at one time? (Pangea) When were they created? (Gen. 10)

† Study the history of geology. Note the different beliefs through the ages. When did scientists' beliefs begin to change? When did scientists begin to doubt Creation? Compare the different periods of time (the 17th, 18th, 19th, and 20th centuries). Make a timeline of the different scientists who contributed to Creation science.

† Study and read about different geologists and scientists throughout history. Write a biographical sketch of one scientist. (250 words)

† Study Egyptian history. What pharaoh built a temple to a sun god, and what was its significance?

† Study ancient history of the Mayans, Incas, Aztecs, Chinese, Greeks, Sumerians, Indians, etc. Do any of these cultures have a story about a great flood?

† Research what the following scientists had to say about the properties of light: Sir Isaac Newton, James Maxwell, Albert Einstein, Benjamin Franklin, and Thomas Edison. Explain how each of their thoughts on the matter shaped or influenced their work. Variation of this activity: Briefly describe in 100 words or less the country in which they lived, the time in which they lived, and several other notable discoveries of each.

† Using the Bible and other sources map out a timeline from Adam to Abraham, then from Abraham to Joshua. List the important events from this time.

† Many times in history events seem to repeat themselves. We should learn from past events so that we do not make the same mistakes. List some of these recurring events. Use sources of early history or Biblical events.

† God uses the word "covenant" in Scripture to describe the relationship between Himself and His people. Do a word search of Scripture and find the number of times it is mentioned in the Old Testament. Write a brief summary of your findings. What can we learn about a covenant with the Lord? How can we apply this to our lives? Explain the New Covenant in your own words.

† Many major, highly degreed scientists of today claim that the Biblical account of Creation is accurate. Research this and list 10-15 of these scientists using websites to aid you.

† Historically people have believed in the literal interpretation of the Creation account. At what time in history did this begin to change? What was happening at the time that may have attributed to this?

† What geologic areas are known for the abundance of fossilized dinosaur bones? Research this and use a world map to chart some of these locations. Does there appear to be a pattern? Locate the major oil-producing areas.

† Plan and take a trip. Using maps of the different areas, plot your course. If you have your driver's license, get permission to drive for part of the journey. Stop at places of interest and take photographs along the way. Create a photographic display of your trip.

† As you are taking a trip across the countryside, look for road cuts (areas where road construction has cut through a hill or mountain and sedimentary layers are exposed) and stop to examine them. Keep a journal of rock layers you have examined.

† Make a map of Australia. Include the coastal regions that are heavily populated, the desert interior region, and their own salt lake. Note famous rocks such as Ayers Rock, also known as Uluru. Be sure to include an index and scale.

† Study and write a report on the life of Blaise Pascal, one of the great early mathematicians. He is considered to be the father of hydrodynamics, and he laid the foundations for differential calculus and probability. What was his *Pensées*? Evaluate the Wager of Pascal.

† Charles Lyell is considered to be the father of the principle of uniformitarianism. Search online for Lyell and his book, *Principles of Geology,* which he wrote even though he was not a geologist, but rather a lawyer. How did he influence Charles Darwin?

† Study the life and accomplishments of Johannes Kepler who was a devoted Christian. He founded the study of astronomy and discovered the laws of planetary motion.

† George Washington Carver was a Christian who was born a slave. He went on to develop over 300 products from the humble peanut. Research other notable Christian inventors who discovered or invented amazing products.

† There are governmental sites such as the United States Geographical Services that provide free online maps. Type in the keyword "geological maps" and look for this site as well as others. Research areas we have studied in this unit.

† Locate Mt. Ararat on a map. In what country is it located? Research this locale and its current inhabitants.

Art/Music
9-12

Art

† Study the history of art in the 17th, 18th, 19th, and 20th centuries.

† Make a wordless picture of the days of Creation. Draw different scenes in small frames.

† Use colored chalk on construction paper to make an abstract drawing of Creation. Use black paper for a neat effect.

† Sand Art. God created man out of the dust of the earth. You can create art from the "earth" using fine, clean sand. Supplies: white glue in a squeeze container, stiff cardboard (any size), clean sand, colored powders such as powdered poster paint, ground spices, corn meal, crushed charcoal, or grated colored chalk (you may use food coloring, but it takes time for colored sand to dry before you can use it). Make an assortment of colored sand. Brush lightly watered-down glue all over a piece of cardboard and sprinkle with plain sand. Give the cardboard a tap to shake off the loose sand particles. Let dry. Paint designs directly on the background with glue (one color at a time), and sprinkle the colored sand on each. Shake off and spray the entire work with a matte fixative (outdoors) if desired.

† Pressed flower art. The beauty of God's Creation is all around us. What better way than nature walks and observing to appreciate His awesome works? While walking you may wish to pick some wildflowers or use flowers from your own garden. Select flowers, blossoms, leaves, ferns, or grasses. Afternoon is the best time to pick these items, since fresh and dry blooms work best. (See directions for pressing flowers on page 142.) Glue the pressed flowers in an arrangement on a piece of heavy paper. Once the entire picture is dry, cover it with a piece of clear contact paper. Variation: make a bookmark.

† Pressed flowers may be used to decorate candles. Glue the flowers on a thick candle. Once they are dry, paint a layer of slightly watered-down glue over the entire candle. Allow to dry. This makes a great gift!

† In the times of Adam and Eve, Noah, and many generations beyond, retail stores were nonexistent. Everything needed had to be harvested, gathered, or created from items found in nature. Baskets or other carrying devices were created and often left behind once the people moved from one place to another, since they took up space and could be easily created in another location. In the spirit of the early people, make a salt-dough basket. Create a salt dough mixture. (See materials list on page 142 for directions.) Turn a bread pan upside down and cover the outside surface with cooking oil. Roll the salt dough out on a generously floured surface, about ¼ inch thick. Cut the dough into ¾-inch strips with a ruler and knife or pizza cutter. Lay 5-6 strips across the bread pan vertically. Then lay 2-3 strips horizontally, weaving them over and under the cross pieces. Weave 2 strips around

the sides of the pan. Hold the strips in place by wetting the dough with a small amount of water where 2 strips come together. Press the dough firmly but gently. Cut the excess off at the bottom of the pan. Roll some dough into a very long rope and wind it around the pan right at the bottom where the strips end. Moisten the ends of the strips to help them stick to the dough rope. Let the basket dry at room temperature (3 days) or bake it in a 325-degree oven for one hour. Let cool completely. Remove the basket by carefully lifting it off the bread pan. Seal the basket with a coat of varnish to strengthen and protect it from moisture. Brush on an acrylic varnish or spray the basket with artists' fixative. Always use a towel in the basket before placing any food products in it to serve.

† Braided Rope Activity: Another activity to demonstrate how to use what is available to "make do" or create useful items. Use strips of scrap fabric or buy cheap remnants. Cut the fabric into ½-inch-wide strips around 3 feet long. Tie or sew 3 strips together at one end, then braid the strips. Do this with different colors or select a color theme. Once you have 9 feet or more, begin with the first length of braided material and begin wrapping it into a tight circle. Using strong double thread, sew the fabric coil together as you roll it. You can make a rug, small trivets for the table, or other decorative items for the house.

† Braid rope from natural products. Research the Native American Indians, especially the Seminole tribe. Study the techniques they used to braid rope. These braided ropes were very fragile-looking but very strong and were used to make fish nets among many other uses.

† Study some of the great artists that God has gifted with astounding talent. Look at the works of Leonardo da Vinci, Michelangelo, and others. Notice their greatest works are on religious themes. Leonardo da Vinci is known for painting the *Mona Lisa,* but did you know he is also the artist of *The Last Supper*? Michelangelo is known for painting the ceiling of the Sistine Chapel, but he also was the sculptor of the *Pietà,* the statue depicting Jesus being held by his mother after the crucifixion. Research other artists of this time period.

† Cave dwellers are said to have drawn pictures on the walls of caves. They were considered primitive men by some anthropologists due to the fallacies of the belief in evolution. Creationists, on the other hand, believe that these people were descendants of Noah and may have fled to caves after the tower of Babel incident. Research the art of cave dwellers and the beauty and intricacies of this form of art. Also, do a word search (cave dwellers, or primitive man) on a Creationist website and read the information provided.

† Observe the beauty of symmetry in God's Creation. You can observe geometric shapes in many of the structures found outdoors. Some trees have rectangular trunks and oval or round branches. Cut out various geometric designs from magazines and make a landscape or still life. Try to use your artistic imagination; if you are lacking in this area, just copy the designs of our Creator.

† Use magazine, newspaper, or junk mail to make a montage or collage. You can cut out

letters, sayings, or objects. Glue this to a colored piece of paper or a blank sheet.

† Try making art from recyclable containers. One lady became famous for her recyclable creations. For example, coffee cans which are painted or covered with contact paper can become pencil holders, plant vases, etc. Use your imagination.

Music

† Study the history of music in the 17th, 18th, 19th, and 20th centuries. (*A Taste for the Classics* comes with a CD of classical music.)

† Study the composers' lives. (See *A Taste for the Classics*.)

† Compose a song. Use a poem you have written and set it to music. Use different musical instruments or sing. Try to use a style similar to a composer you have studied. Use this song to give glory to God for His magnificent Creation!

† The beauty of music can be defined mathematically. Research and explain the tones on a scale. What is pleasing to the ear?

† What happens to music if the beat is off or a key is misplayed? Explain how orderliness is imperative to making music. How does this fit in with the orderliness of God? Can we see His hand in everything?

† Research the various musical instruments. Which instruments are used in an orchestra? What types of instruments are used in a band? What is the difference between an orchestra and a band?

† Take a music appreciation class or research the various types of music. What are the historical origins of various types of music such as jazz, contemporary, or rock? What type of negative connotations do some types of music hold? Why is this?

† Listen to various musical pieces and try to discern the types of instruments that are playing. Use a computer or online program that will allow you to easily find the answer!

† Picture a tune. Draw a diagram of a musical bar of your favorite song or a familiar tune. Look at the diagram. What does it show you? Can you see the variations of the patterns in the music?

Resources
Books / Video / Computer

The Beginning of the World by Dr. Henry Morris (Master Books, 1991, 184 pages). God is calling more and more scientists to defend the faith, and the result is a surge of awareness that the Bible is true after all. Examined are the historical and scientific aspects of the literal six-day Creation, a young earth, and the worldwide catastrophic Flood of Noah.

The Biblical Basis for Modern Science by Dr. Henry Morris (Baker Books, 1986, 516 pages). A textbook on Creationism for anyone who wants to study a complete overview of the subject. This book covers twelve major disciplines of science and Biblical passages dealing with each field.

Bone of Contention by Sylvia Baker (Evangelical Press, 1993, 35 pages).Very good overview of Creation and evolution. Refutes scientific arguments used by evolutionists.

Bones of Contention by Marvin L. Lubenow (Baker Book House, 1973, revised 2001, 295 pages). A Creationist assessment of human fossils written for the layperson. The evidence is based entirely on fossils accepted unconditionally by evolutionist.

The Collapse of Evolution by Scott M. Huse (Baker Books, 1983, 208 pages). This book exposes the flaws in evolutionary theory with fascinating examples of design in our world.

Considering God's Creation by Susan Mortimer and Betty Smith (Eagle's Wings, 1998, 128 pages). Excellent way to introduce your children to the God's awesome Creation!

Creation and the Second Coming by Dr. Henry Morris (Master Books, 1991, 194 pages). To understand the end, you must understand the beginning. In this book Dr. Henry Morris shows how Creation is tied to the Second Coming of Christ.

Creation Facts of Life by Dr. Gary Parker (Master Books, 1994, 215 pages). Dr. Gary Parker made the transition from evolutionist to Creationist after three years of examining evidence.

Creation Rediscovered: Evolution and the Importance of the Origins Debate by Gerard J. Keane (TAN Books, 1999, 398 pages). A resource of major significance to the Catholic Christian. Discusses the basic question of evolution, the discoveries of science, the problem with evolution for a Christian, the influence of evolutionary belief systems in our world, and more. For high school and above.

Darwin's Black Box by Michael Behe (The Free Press, 1996, 307 pages). A microbiologist and homeschool dad concentrates on the evidences of Creation in the unseen world.

Darwin's Enigma by Luther Sunderland (Master Books, 1988, 180 pages). Darwin's theory of evolution has not gone away, even though no fossil evidence to support his theory has surfaced. Based on interviews with directors of the world's leading fossil museums.

Dinosaurs, The Lost World, and You by John D. Morris, Ph.D. (Master Books, 1999, 48 pages). A brief look at how dinosaurs fit into the Creation model.

Evolution: The Challenge of the Fossil Record by Dr. Duane Gish (Creation Life Resources, Master Books, 1985, 277 pages). After defining the evolution and Creation models of origins, the author takes a hard look at the fossil record and its lack of proof for evolution.

Fossils Facts and Fantasies by Joe Taylor (Mt. Blanco Publishing Co., 2001, 80 pages). Learn from one of the best in the field. Joe Taylor is well known in the paleontological world for his expertise in fossil excavation with a Creationist twist. This book is beautifully illustrated and very entertaining.

Genesis for Kids: Science Experiments That Show God's Power in Creation! by Doug Lambier and Robert Stevenson (Tommy Nelson, Inc., 1988, 160 pages). A fantastic experiment book dealing with the days of Creation. All seven days are covered with activities to challenge K-8th grade.

God Created...Sea Life of the World, Animals of the World, Dinosaurs of the World, etc. Master Books, 1989, 32 pages each). A series of five coloring books with beautifully illustrated colored stickers to place on corresponding pages. A great addition for young children K-6. Informative and fun.

In the Minds of Men by Ian Taylor (TFE Publishing, 1991, 438 pages). One of the most popular layman's books available on evolutionary history and thinking. Especially suitable for high school students.

It Couldn't Just Happen by Lawrence O. Richards (Word Publishing, 1987, 191 pages). Our children are constantly bombarded with evolution as a "fact." The Lord has given us thousands of evidences to prove His Creation. This book fascinates kids with examples of God's works.

Many Infallible Proofs by Dr. Henry Morris (Master Books, 1974, 381 pages). This book shows that the Bible is historically and scientifically dependable.

Men of Science/Men of God by Dr. Henry Morris (Master Books, second ed., 1988, 107 pages). Over 100 mini-biographies of great scientists of the past and present who believed in the Creator.

The Puzzle of Ancient Man (Advanced Technology in Past Civilizations?) by Donald E. Chittick (Creation Compass, 1998, 182 pages). A fantastic example of information confounding scientists of today. This book makes a compelling argument for man being created with intelligence as God designed.

Streams of Civilization, Volume One by Albert Hyma and Mary Stanton (Creation-Life Publishers, 1992, 410 pages). A very good and comprehensive romp through history from the dawn of the world to A.D. 1294! This book is written from a Creationist perspective and was sponsored by the Institute for Creation Research. A must-have.

Teaching Science through Art: A Science Supplement by Rich and Sharon Jeffus (Visual Manna, 1996, 166 pages). This is an awesome tool to bring art into your science curriculum. Based on many years of combined art experience, this book can inspire your reluctant or aspiring artist. Very clearly written with illustrations throughout. (www.visualmanna.com)

What Is Creation Science? by Dr. Henry Morris and Dr. Gary Parker (Master Books, 1982, 330 pages). This book shows conclusively that Creationism is a viable scientific concept from the evidence available, using Biblical references. An excellent overview of the science of Creation.

Additional Resources

Children's Atlas, ed. Elizabeth Wyse (Dorling Kindersley, 2000).

The Doubleday Children's Atlas of World History, ed. Jane Oliver (McNally, 1987).

Geography From A to Z by Jack Knowlton (HarperCollins, 1988).

Janice Van Cleave's Earth Science for Every Kid by Janice Van Cleave (John Wiley & Sons, 1991).

Jehovah's Park versus Jurassic Park by Catie Frates (Media Angels, 2002). Learn amazing information about dinosaurs and their place in God's creation. Beautiful illustrations by the late Richard Jeffus of Visual Manna.

Let the Authors Speak by Carolyn Hatcher (Old Pinnacle Publishing, 1992).

Maps and Globes by Jack Knowlton (Thomas Y. Crowell Publishing, 1985).

Math Wizardry for Kids by Margaret Kenda and Phyllis S. Williams (Barron's Educational Series, Inc., 1995).

Ranger Rick's NatureScope Geology: The Active Earth (The National Wildlife Federation: 1989). These books are written from an evolutionary point of view yet the activities may be completed without discussing this. The books are available in most libraries.

A Taste for the Classics by Patrick Kavanaugh (Sparrow Press, 1993, 244 pages). A lively guide that describes and walks you through hundreds of masterworks—for hours of reading and listening enjoyment. Includes a music CD.

The Usborne Story of Music by Eileen O'Brien (Usborne / EDC Publishing, 1989).

Audio Cassettes and CDs

Visit www.AnswersinGenesis.org for CDs and cassettes featuring Buddy Davis. Various songs are based on Creation.

Back to Genesis CD-ROMs from the Institute for Creation Research (www.icr.org). Each CD consists of one-minute sound bites from radio programs. These CDs are very informative.

Computer Software

God Created the Birds (Standard Publishing, 1998).

God Created the World and the Universe (Standard Publishing, 1998).

God's A-Z Creatures (Standard Publishing, 1998).

Multilingual Bible Story: Creation, Noah's Ark, Moses (Pine Nut Publishing, 1997).

Internet

Institute for Creation Research (ICR), Dr. John Morris, President, www.icr.org.

Answers in Genesis, Ken Ham, www.answersingenesis.org.

Awesome Works, Dennis Petersen, www.awesomeworks.com.

The Creation Research Society, www.creationresearchsociety.org.

Creation Tour Ministries, www.creationtours.com.

Creation, Dinosaurs, and the Flood, www.sixdaycreation.com.

Creationism Organization, www.creationism.org.

Creation Sensation, www.creationsensation.com.

Creation moments   www.creationmoments.com

Discovery Channel online (info on evolution), www.school.discovery.com.

Media Angels® Inc., www.MediaAngels.com. Great links to many Creation sites.

Videos and DVDs

Creation Adventure Team (Answers in Genesis; www.answersingenesis.org). *A Jurassic Ark Mystery* and *Six Short Days, One Big Adventure*. These entertaining shows depict Creation themes in action-adventure movies. Approximately 30 minutes each.

Icons of Evolution: The Growing Scientific Controversy over Darwin (ColdWater Media, Inc.; www.coldwatermedia.com).

Kent Hovind Creation Science Seminar (www.drdino.com). Complete 11-hour Creation science seminar; videos or CD and workbooks.

Newton's Workshop: The Name Game (Moody Video; www.moodyvideo.org). Animal classification. Many titles in the series. Older elementary.

Unlocking the Mystery of Life: The Scientific Case for Intelligent Design (Illustra Media; www.illustramedia.com).

The following may be ordered through the Institute for Creation Research (www.icr.org):

The Adventures of Marty videos: *Marty's Fossil Adventure, Marty and the Last Dinosaur, Marty's Grand Adventure*

D is for Dinosaur (Answers in Genesis). Letters of the alphabet for younger children.

Dinosaur Mystery Solved.

Grand Canyon: Monument to the Flood.

Incredible Creatures That Defy Evolution I and II.

Mount St. Helens: Explosive Evidence for Catastrophe!

The Origin of the Universe

The Riddle of Origins Set

Additional Resources

Creation Resources		
Creation Studies Institute Tom DeRosa	2401 West Cypress Creek Road Fort Lauderdale, FL 33309	954-315-4310 FAX: (954) 315-7559 www.csinfo.org
Institute for Creation Research Dr. John Morris, President	P.O. Box 1606 El Cajon, CA 92022	619-448-0900 800-628-7640 Fax: 619-448-3469 www.icr.org
Answers in Genesis Ken Ham	P.O. Box 6330 Florence, KY 41022	800-778-3390 www.answersingenesis.org
Awesome Works Dennis Petersen	P.O. Box 570 El Dorado CA 95623	866-225-5229 Fax (530) 626-3221 www.creationresource.org
Creation Science Seminar on Video Kent Hovind	29 Cummings Rd. Pensacola, FL 32503	904-479-DINO (3466) www.drdino.com
Censored Science Catie Frates	P.O. Box 457 Morriston, FL 32668	www.catiefrates.com
Homeschool Science Resources		
Home Training Tools	546 S 18th St W Suite B Billings, MT 59102	800-860-6272 406-256-0990 www.hometrainingtools.com
Tobin's Lab	Tobin's Lab P.O. Box 725 Culpepper, VA 22701	800-522-4776 540-937-7173 www.TobinsLab.com
Science Supply Resources:		
Nasco Science Materials and resources	901 Janesville Ave. Ft. Atkinson, WI 53538-0901	800-558-9595 www.enasco.com
Delta Education Materials and resources	P.O. Box 950 Hudson, NH 03051	800-442-5444 www.delta-education.com

Materials List

Here are some of the materials you may need:

	art paper
	balloons
	beakers or containers with metric measurements
	colored pencils
	compass
	candles
	crayons
	food coloring
	liquid starch
	magnifying glass
	markers
	measuring tape, ruler
	paint
	plastic bags
	plaster of Paris
	poster board
	protractor
	recyclable jars, trays, tubs, etc.
	ruler
	sand
	saucepan
	scissors
	shoestring
	straws
	string
	spiral-bound blank book (no lines)
	tape
	vinegar
	world map

Recipe for salt dough: (Do not bake this dough.) Dough recipe: one cup of flour, one cup of water, one cup of salt, two and one-half teaspoons of cream of tartar, one tablespoon of cooking oil. Mix all ingredients in a saucepan. Cook over medium-low heat. Stir until the dough clumps together and pulls away from the pan. Turn out onto a cutting board and knead when cool. You may tint this dough with food coloring. This mixture can be reused and will stay pliable if it is kept in a sealed container. (Do not bake this dough!)

Recipe for salt dough #2: (May be baked and painted.) 1 cup of salt, 2 cups of white four, 1 cup of water. Mix well in a bowl and turn out on a flat surface and knead with your fingers for 5-7 minutes. It shouldn't stick to the table. If it does sprinkle four on the work surface until the dough pulls clean. Keep in a plastic bag or covered bowl so it won't dry out. Keeps for 5 days.

Directions for flower press: Afternoon is the best time to pick items to press. Fresh, dry blooms work best. Place the plants between sheets of clean paper, then place them between the pages of a fat book or plant press. Press the plants for 1-2 weeks until they are completely dry. Lay out the pressed plants and handle carefully. Use these for various crafts. May be stored (1-3 days) between layers of wax paper in a box.

Materials Chart

Items Needed	Purchase	Collect from home

Field Trip Ideas

You may wish to research areas in your location which include field trips led by Creation scientists. There are probably more than you think! Here are a few to choose from:

Attend a Creation science seminar:

Many wonderful, highly degreed speakers travel the globe to bring updated information about the origins debate. Of course our own Jill Whitlock is available! Contact her at www.MediaAngels.com. Check local listings via the internet at www.icr.org, www.answersingenesis.org and www.csinfo.org

Creation Based Tours: See additional resources on p. 135 for contact information.
     ICR hosts tours of the Grand Canyon and Mt. St. Helens.
     Answers in Genesis hosts tours of the Grand Canyon.

Paleontological Digs:

Check your local newspaper, nature centers, library, universities, or Creation organizations for more information about available digs in your area.

These Creation based-digs were available at the time of this printing:

Creation Studies Institute: The semi-annual Fossil Float on the Peace River takes place in Arcadia, Florida. Mammoth bones as well as many other amazing remains have been uncovered with this group. Call 1-800-882-0278 or check online at www.csinfo.org.

Creation Expeditions: Digs are currently offered in Colorado, the Peace River, and ecology from a Creationist perspective in Crystal Springs, Florida. Contact the DeRosas at 352-795-1308 or www.creationexpeditions.com

Museums:

Institute for Creation Research: ICR Museum of Creation and Earth History is a wonderful place to learn first-hand information about origins. See Additional Resources on p.140 for contact information.

Traveling museums: Tom Baird has been named a lecturer for Answers in Genesis and is the curator of Noah's Park, a unique museum that consists of dinosaur fossils and scale models. It is a great educational tool that encourages children's interest in Creation.

STARLAB is a unique portable planetarium that Tom uses to explain the awesomeness of God's Creation! He has developed a unique program using STARLAB that focuses around the Gospel in the stars. Interested in hosting his traveling museum? Contact Tom Baird at Noah's Park and Planetarium, P.O. Box 35, Christmas, FL 32709. Phone: 407-568-5165.

Science field trips with a guide:

Bill and Merilee Clifton, Science Partners: Florida-based workshops and field trips hosted by the Cliftons. www.sciencepartners.net.

Museum field trips online:

Creation Sensations has an online museum website. Updated regularly, this site ensures education and enjoyment. www.creationsensation.com

Enjoy educational fieldtrips online, www.Virtual-Field-Trips.com, travel without leaving your home. Updated with new field trips each month many in the area of science.

Science Experiment

Title:

Question:

Hypothesis:

Materials:

Procedure:

Observation/Data:

Conclusion:

Science Experiment

Title:

Question: (What is the experiment about?)

My Guess: (What do I think will happen?)

Materials: (What I used)

What happened?

BEFORE PICTURE	AFTER PICTURE

Why did it happen?

SCIENCE EXPERIMENT

TITLE OF MY EXPERIMENT

_____

Question: (What is the experiment about?)

My Guess: (What do I think will happen?)

Materials: (What I used)

What I did:

What happened?

Why did it happen?

Scientific Method

Title:

Question:

Hypothesis:

Materials:

Procedure:

Observation/Data:

Conclusion:

References

Ackerman, Paul D. 1993. *It's A Young World After All: Exciting Evidences for Recent Creation.* Grand Rapids, Mich.: Baker Books.

Akridge, Russell. 1980. *The Sun Is Shrinking.* Impact article 82. Institute for Creation Research.

Austin, S. A. and D. R. Humphreys. 1991. "The Sea's Missing Salt: A Dilemma for Evolutionists." *Proceedings of the Second International Conference on Creationism*, 2.

Austin, Steve. 1994. *Grand Canyon: Monument to Catastrophe.* Santee, Calif.: Institute of Creation Research.

Bliss, Richard B., 1988. *Origins—Creation or Evolution.* El Cajon, Calif.: Master Books.

Brown, Walt. 1995. *In the Beginning: Compelling Evidence for Creation and the Flood.* Phoenix, Ariz.: Center for Scientific Creation.

Clark, Robert T., and James D. Bales. 1966. *Why Scientists Accept Evolution.* Grand Rapids, Mich.: Baker Book House.

Creation. 2003. 25, no. 3:7.

Crick, Francis. 1988. *What Mad Pursuit: A Personal View of Scientific Discovery.* N.Y.: Basic Books.

Darwin, Charles. 1859. *On the Origin of Species.* www.infidels.org/library/historical/Charles_Darwin/origins.html.

Fields, Weston, W. 1976. *Unformed and Unfilled: A Critique to the Gap Theory.* Collinsville, Ill.: Burgener Entertainment.

Flamsteed, Sam. 1995. "Crisis in the Cosmos." *Discover* 16, no. 3. March, 1995, pp. 80-90.

Forey, Peter. 2003. Review of *Genetics, Paleontology and Macroevolution* by Jeffrey Levington, *Journal of Paleontology* 77, no. 1.

Gentry, Robert V. 1995. *Creation's Tiny Mystery.* Knoxville, Tenn.: Earth Science Association.

Grigg, Russell. 1993. "The Mind of God and the Big Bang." *Creation ex nihilo* 15, no. 4:38-43.

Grigg, Russell. 1996. "Ernst Haeckel—Evangelist for Evolution and Apostle of Deceit." *Creation ex nihilo* 18, no. 2:33-36.

Grigg, Russell. 1998. "Fraud Rediscovered." *Creation ex nihilo* 20, no. 2:49-51.

Ham, Ken. 1993. "I Got Excited at Mt. St. Helen's." *Creation ex nihilo* 15, no. 3:14-19.

Humphreys, Russell. 1995. *Starlight and Time: Solving the Puzzle of Distant Starlight in a Young Universe.* Colorado Springs, Colo.: Master Books.

Johnson, Phillip E. 1991 *Darwin on Trial.* Downers Grove, Ill.: InterVarsity Press.

Johnson, Robert Bowie, Jr. 2002. *Athena and Eden: The Hidden Meaning of the Parthenon's East Façade.* Annapolis, MD.: Solving Light Books.

Johnson, Robert Bowie, Jr. 2003. *Athena and Kain: The True Meaning of Greek Myth.* Annapolis, MD.: Solving Light Books.

Juhasz, David. 1996. "The Incredible Woodpecker." *Creation ex nihilo* 18, no. 1. pp. 10-13.

Kausman, Leslie, and Sara NcGrath, et al 1996. "Welcome to the Club." *Newsweek*, 23 December, 52.

Lemonick, Michael B. and J. Madeleine Nash. 1995. "When Did the Universe Begin?" *Time,* 6 March, 76-84.

Matthews, Mike. "Space Life? Answering Unearthly Allegations." *Creation* 25, no. 3:55. June-Aug 2003

Mehlert, A. W. 1999. "The Rise and Fall of Skull KNM-ER 1470." *Creation ex nihilo* 13, no.2. www.trueorigins.org/skull1470.asp.

Moore, John N. 1997. "I Used to Be Darwin's Disciple." *Decision,* January.

Morris, Henry M. 1985. *Scientific Creationism.* El Cajon, Calif.: Master Books.

Morris, Henry M. 1991. *The Beginning of the World*. El Cajon, Calif.: Master Books.

Morris, Henry M., and Gary E. Parker. 1987. *What Is Creation Science?* El Cajon, Calif.: Master Books.

Morris, Henry M., and John C. Whitcomb. 1961. *The Genesis Flood.* Philadelphia, Pa.: Presbyterian and Reformed Publishing Co.

Morris, Henry M. & John D. Morris. 1989. *Science, Scripture, and the Young Earth.* El Cajon, Calif.: Institute for Creation Research.

Morris, John. 1993. "Was There Really An Ice Age?" Back To Genesis, #56b August, 1993.

Morris, John D. 1994. *The Young Earth.* El Cajon, Calif.: Master Books.

Morris, John D., ed. 2003. *Acts and Facts.* El Cajon, Calif.: Institute for Creation Resarch.

National Geographic. 1975. Map of the Physical World. *National Geographic* 148:5.

Norman, T. G. and Barry Setterfield. 1990. *Atomic Constants, Light and Time.* Sunnybank, QLD, Australia: Creation Science Foundation Ltd.

Oard, Michael J. 1990. *An Ice Age Caused by the Genesis Flood.* El Cajon, Calif.: Institute of Creation Research.

Palmer, Trevor. 1999. "Controversy—Catastrophism & Evolution." *Kluwer Academic October,* 266. 470pp.

Patten, Donald W. 1973. *The Biblical Flood and the Ice Epoch.* Seattle, Wash.: Pacific Meridian Publishing Co.

Peebles, James, and David Schram, et al. 1994. "The Evolution of the Universe." *Scientific American* 271, no. 4:52-57.

Petersen, Dennis R. 1990. *Unlocking the Mysteries of Creation.* El Dorado, Calif.: Creation Resource Foundation.

Sarfati, Jonathan. 1998. "The Moon: The Light That Rules the Night." *Creation ex nihilo* 20, no. 4:36-39.

Setterfield, Barry. *The Velocity of Light and the Age of the Universe.* Creation Science Australia: Foundation Ltd..

Snelling, Andrew. 1989. "Part 4: The Matter of the Shrinking Sun." *Creation ex nihilo* 11, no. 4:45-47.

Steele, Dewitt. 1983. *Science of the Physical Creation in Christian Perspective* Pensacola, Fla.: A Beka Book Publications.

Steidl, P.F. 1983. "Planets, Comets, and Asteroids." *Design and Origins in Astronomy,* 73-106.

Stokes, William L., and Sheldon Judson. 1968. *Introduction to Geology.* Englewood Cliffs, N.J.: Prentice-Hall, Inc.

Thompson, Bert. 1986. *The Scientific Case for Creation.* Montgomery, Ala.: Apologetics Press, Inc.

Thornton, Joseph and Rob DeSalle. 2000. "Geneomics Meets Phylogenetics." *Annual Review of Genomics and Human Genetics,* 64.

Vago, R., E. Gill, and J. C. Collingwood. 1997. "Laser Measurements of Coral Growth." *Nature* 386:30-31.

Vardiman, Larry. 1996. *Sea-Floor Sediment and the Age of the Earth.* El Cajon, Calif.: Institute for Creation Research.

Wieland, Carl. 1995. "Surtsey, The Young Island That Looks Old." *Creation ex nihilo* 17, no. 2:10-12.

Wong, J. T. 2003. "The Big Bang Theory Busts." In http://web.uvic.ca/~jtwong/bigbang.htm [cited 29 September 2003].

More Media Angels Books

Visit us online: www.MediaAngels.com
www.Virtual-Field-Trips.com

Order online or send check for book price plus 6% tax (FL residents only) and 15% shipping (US orders only) to Media Angels®, Inc., 15720 S. Pebble Lane, Ft. Myers, FL 33912.

Creation Science Unit Studies by Felice Gerwitz and Jill Whitlock $18.95 each
Each fantastic study guide is written from a Biblical Creationist perspective, on three levels spanning K-12. Includes a teaching outline, activities, experiments, activities, resources, reproducible sheets, and much more. These resources will help you with all the planning you need to teach the wonders of God's Creation!

> *Creation Geology: A Study Guide to Fossils, Formations and the Flood!*
> *Creation Anatomy: A Study Guide to the Miracles of the Body!*
> *Creation Astronomy: A Study Guide to the Constellations!*

Science Hands-On Experiment and Activity Pack by Felice Gerwitz, $12.95 each
Thess packs contain ready-to-copy activities and experiments, directions, scientific method sheets, games and crossword puzzles, glossary, and much more. This resource complements the unit study guides. Choose Geology & Creation Science, Anatomy, or Astronomy.

Teaching Science and Having Fun! by Felice Gerwitz, $12.95
This handy teacher's reference includes how to schedule, what to teach, a scope and sequence, the scientific method, how to set up a lab, how to choose a microscope, resources, and much more. Felice—a former classroom teacher—has homeschooled since 1986, holds science workshops for children, and conducts seminars for adults.

An Insider's Guide to Successful Science Fair Projects by Felice Gerwitz, $6.50
A handy guide for helping parents and children put together a winning Science Fair Project! Great science fair strategies, how to plan, where to look for information, the scientific method, keeping a journal, writing a report and abstract, display guidelines, what judges look for, and much more.

Virtual Field Trips: An Online Study Guide by Felice Gerwitz, $18.95
Take a virtual trip in the comfort of your own home. Fun field trips are mapped out for you with scavenger hunt questions to answer along the way. This is a wonderful supplement to your home education. Learn how to use the internet to enhance your unit studies.

***Truth Seekers Mystery Series*™** by Felice Gerwitz and Christina Gerwitz; Creation-based adventure novels for the entire family. You've studied the topic of Creation, now read the books! These faith-filled teen mystery stories will delve into the basic arguments evolutionists use in "proving" their position. Teaches students how to answer these questions in a fun to read, adventure story. You will want to collect the series. Join homeschooled teens Christian and Anna Murphy and their family as they face action, adventure, mystery, and heart-stopping suspense and learn that the truth will set you free! Current titles: *The Missing Link: Found*, $7.99; *Dinosaur Quest at Diamond Peak*, $7.99; *Keys to the Past: Unlocked*, $8.99.

***Truth Seekers Mystery Series*™ Literature Study Guides** by Felice Gerwitz $6.50 each
These easy-to-use literature study guides bring the science-based novels to life. Help budding writers in your home study literary techniques in a nonthreatening way. Check for reading and vocabulary comprehension and then study the additional science topics explored in the novels. Easy to use and fun to study! Current titles: *Literature Study Guide: Missing Link Found, Dinosaur Quest at Diamond Peak, and Keys to the Past Unlocked.*

About the Authors

Felice Gerwitz is a former teacher with a degree in Elementary Education, Learning Disabilities, and Early Childhood Education. She grew up in a family that knew the Lord. When taught evolution in junior high school, she asked her mother who was right. Her mother answered, "The Bible!" Since meeting Jill, Felice has a better understanding of Creation Science! She has homeschooled since 1986 and has five children. Felice is owner of Media Angels®, Inc., along with her husband Jeff. Questions? e-mail: MediAngels@aol.com.

Jill Whitlock believed that evolution was the way life and the world began. She was trained as an evolutionist and worked as a geologist for ten years after graduating from Texas A & M University. She worked as Chief Well Log Analyst for the Rocky Mountain Region and as Senior Staff Exploration Geologist for an oil company in Denver, Colorado. Jill accepted the Lord Jesus Christ as Savior in 1984 and began praying and studying about the Creation-versus-evolution question. The Lord was faithful and brought many people into her path who started her on the way to becoming a Flood Geologist and a Young Earth Creationist. Jill has since been studying and compiling information on Creation Science. She has been homeschooling her three boys since 1986, two of whom have graduated and the third son will shortly. Jill holds Creation science seminars and workshops and is available for speaking. Write to Jill at: whitlock@sprynet.com.